Transmedia Storytelling

D1114200

Transmedia Storytelling

The Librarian's Guide

Amanda S. Hovious

LIBRARIES
UNLIMITED™
An Imprint of ABC-CLIO, LLC
Santa Barbara, California • Denver, Colorado

Copyright © 2016 by Amanda S. Hovious

All rights reserved. No part of this publication may be reproduced, stored in a retrieval system, or transmitted, in any form or by any means, electronic, mechanical, photocopying, recording, or otherwise, except for the inclusion of brief quotations in a review, without prior permission in writing from the publisher.

Library of Congress Cataloging-in-Publication Data

Names: Hovious, Amanda S., author.
Title: Transmedia storytelling : the librarian's guide / Amanda
    S. Hovious.
Description: Santa Barbara, CA : Libraries Unlimited, an imprint of
    ABC-CLIO, LLC, [2016] | Includes bibliographical references and index.
Identifiers: LCCN 2015025227 | ISBN 9781440838484 (paperback) |
    ISBN 9781440838491 (ebook)
Subjects: LCSH: School libraries—Activity programs. | Digital
    storytelling. | Interactive multimedia. | Storytelling in education. | Mass
    media in education. | Technological literacy—Study and teaching—
    Activity programs. | Children's libraries—Activity programs. | Young
    adults' libraries—Activity programs. | BISAC: LANGUAGE ARTS &
    DISCIPLINES / Library & Information Science / School Media. |
    LANGUAGE ARTS & DISCIPLINES / Library & Information Science /
    Collection Development. | LANGUAGE ARTS & DISCIPLINES /
    Library & Information Science / General.
Classification: LCC Z675.S3 .H675 2016 | DDC 027.62/51—dc23
LC record available at http://lccn.loc.gov/2015025227

ISBN: 978-1-4408-3848-4
EISBN: 978-1-4408-3849-1

20 19 18 17 16   1 2 3 4 5

This book is also available on the World Wide Web as an eBook.
Visit www.abc-clio.com for details.

Libraries Unlimited
An Imprint of ABC-CLIO, LLC

ABC-CLIO, LLC
130 Cremona Drive, P.O. Box 1911
Santa Barbara, California 93116–1911

This book is printed on acid-free paper ∞
Manufactured in the United States of America

Contents

Introduction

Are you interested in innovative programming ideas for your library that connect literacy learning to technology? Then you have come to the right place! Transmedia storytelling—storytelling across multiple media platforms—is a powerful tool for motivating, engaging, and inspiring library users of all ages to read, make, and learn.

From transmedia story times to transmedia fiction clubs to transmedia-inspired library instruction and beyond, this book takes a theory-to-practice approach, resulting in a guide that explores the literacy-rich learning values of transmedia storytelling in Part One (first four chapters), and then puts those theories into practice in Part Two (last two chapters), through transmedia storytelling program ideas that can be implemented in either public or school libraries. The goal of this book is to provide a one-stop shop for everything librarians (and teachers) need to know about transmedia storytelling, along with transmedia-based activities that not only support 21st-century literacies and learning but are also well aligned to 21st-century learning standards—making them both library-ready and classroom adaptable.

Following is an overview for each chapter:

- **Chapter One** lays the groundwork by defining transmedia storytelling and describing successful examples of projects that help bring the concept into sharper focus.

- **Chapter Two** makes connections between literacy theories and the characteristics of transmedia storytelling to explain how transmedia literacy practices can be seen as a new way of reading.

- **Chapter Three** explains how the elements of both storytelling and gameplay make transmedia storytelling a powerful learning tool.

- **Chapter Four** describes how libraries can make transmedia storytelling discoverable, and by doing so can support and promote their missions and goals.

- **Chapter Five** presents seven different types of transmedia storytelling program ideas, with multiple examples and step-by-step instructions.

- **Chapter Six** provides templates and guidance for the transmedia technology planning process.

My inspiration for this book comes from the transmedia storytelling project, *Inanimate Alice*, which I discovered in a game-based learning course. I immediately became smitten with its beauty and literary value, and was equally mesmerized by its literacy-rich affordances. That discovery led to an interest in using projects like *Inanimate Alice* for learning activities within classrooms and libraries.

While first and foremost I define myself as a librarian, I am also a professionally trained instructional designer, and have found those skills incredibly useful for the design and development of the library programs in this book. My hope is that librarians and educators who read this book gain a better understanding of the value of transmedia storytelling as a literacy and learning tool, and are inspired to experiment with the transmedia storytelling program ideas in this book within their own libraries and classrooms.

PART I

Origins, Foundations, and Applications

CHAPTER 1

What Is Transmedia Storytelling?

Origins of the Concept ■ **The Seven Principles of Transmedia Storytelling** ■ **Transmedia Storytelling Types** ■ **Transmedia Storytelling Genres**

Transmedia storytelling takes the traditional art of storytelling to a whole new level, delivering a fictional story across multiple media platforms—whether physical, digital, or both—to create a truly immersive storytelling experience. This chapter explores the origins of transmedia storytelling, the principles that define it, and the different types of transmedia narratives; and ends with case studies of exemplary projects that help to further illustrate the concept of transmedia storytelling.

Origins of the Concept

Media studies scholar Henry Jenkins (2003) introduced the concept of transmedia storytelling in a *Technology Review* article about the collaborative effort of Hollywood and the gaming industry to develop content that could expand the entertainment experience across multiple media platforms. In his definitive work, *Convergence Culture* (2006), Jenkins defined a transmedia story as one that "unfolds across multiple media platforms, with each new text making a distinctive and valuable contribution to the whole" (95–96). Other scholars have taken different approaches to defining transmedia storytelling. Walker (2004) described transmedia storytelling as a theory of distributed narratives—narratives that "explode the work altogether, sending fragments and shards across media, through the network and sometimes into the physical spaces that we live in" (1). Dena (2004) used the term *cross-media storytelling*, emphasizing the central importance of the user and the role of the storyline in the user's activity. Rose (2015) proposed the idea of immersive media, focusing on immersion as a key feature of transmedia storytelling. All these definitions reflect different aspects of transmedia storytelling.

Efforts to expand entertainment experiences across multiple media platforms have long been commonplace in the world of children's entertainment with the merchandising of character-based games, toys, and books (e.g., Pokemon). Today, Hollywood has fully embraced the concept of transmedia storytelling as demonstrated in franchises such as the Lord of the Rings, where the characters of Middle Earth were spun off from the books into blockbuster movies, video games, virtual worlds, music, and merchandise—all of which fuel and satisfy the unquenchable thirst of die-hard fans of the trilogy. Transmedia storytelling is more than just the spin-off of a story or set of characters from one media platform to another though. Each media platform expands and experiments with the story or characters in such a way that inspires the audience to want to further explore different avenues or angles of the story. At the same time, each media platform stands alone, so that the audience may enter the story world at any one point, whether book, movie, or video game. Taken together, the multiple media outlets create a fully immersive storytelling experience that motivates fans to explore all the story worlds (Jenkins 2006).

> **During the immensely popular run of the HBO series, <u>True Blood</u>, social media was heavily embraced as an integral part of the storytelling experience. For example, character Jessica Hamby was given her own weblog where she discussed life as a baby vampire. To maintain the fantasy, other elements of the show had a web presence as well, including a web site and Facebook page for the Fellowship of the Sun.**

It is important to note that not all cross-platform stories qualify as transmedia storytelling, at least according to Jenkins's definition. For example, the adaptation of the <u>Harry Potter</u> series from books to movies does not meet the definition of transmedia storytelling because the movies served to replicate the story rather than retell it or continue it. However, *Pottermore*, a virtual world built around the series, does represent an example of transmedia storytelling because it allows for the audience to immerse itself in the experience of Harry Potter's world in ways outside the original books. In fact, the addition of video games and virtual worlds to Hollywood entertainment franchises has served as a pivotal part of the development of transmedia storytelling. Additionally, technology growth has resulted in new ways to communicate—such as social media—further enabling transmedia storytelling to flourish.

Today, transmedia storytelling has moved beyond the domain of Hollywood producers and game developers. The development of software platforms like Conducttr (conducttr.com) makes the creation of transmedia storytelling projects accessible for just about anyone. By pulling together features such as game mechanics, real-time feedback, voting, badges, and player personalization, Conducttr simplifies the process of transmedia storytelling development, allowing individuals or groups to create immersive storytelling experiences with one tool. This has led to transmedia endeavors by a cross-section of groups, from artists to filmmakers to marketers to educators—all experimenting with the affordances of transmedia storytelling in order to discover ways in which it can be applied to their respective fields. In that sense, transmedia storytelling is still in the process of being shaped, and within each field it may end up being shaped differently, resulting in subtle—and perhaps not so subtle—variations in form. Regardless of the formation that transmedia storytelling takes, to be defined as such, it requires the inclusion of elements from Jenkins's (2009b) seven principles of transmedia storytelling.

The Seven Principles of Transmedia Storytelling

The concept of transmedia storytelling demonstrates the movement toward a new culture of media distribution—one in which the audience plays a participatory role where sharing, remixing, retelling, and reshaping of content is the new norm. Jenkins (2009b) identified seven elements that are inherent to this new way of circulating media content and that illustrate the shift to a participatory culture. They are described as the seven principles of transmedia storytelling:

1. *Spreadability vs. Drillability*. Spreadability refers to the ease in which media content can be circulated, which is determined by a number of factors, including technical affordances, level of restrictions on circulation, and motivation of the audience to share content. Drillability refers to the depth of the audience's engagement in the content.

2. *Continuity vs. Multiplicity*. Continuity refers to the way the narrative is continued across multiple media content. Multiplicity refers to alternative retellings of the story that situate the characters in new plots (e.g., fan fiction).

3. *Immersion vs. Extractability*. Immersion refers to the depth at which the audience is drawn into the story world. Extractability refers to the

elements that the audience takes away from the story to employ in the real world (e.g., cosplay).

4. *World building*. World building refers to the ways in which the story world intersects with the audience's daily life (e.g., fictional travel posters).

5. *Seriality*. Seriality refers to the way in which transmedia storytelling delivers the story across multiple media outlets in chunks, much in the way a series is continued across a single media platform.

6. *Subjectivity*. Subjectivity refers to the way in which transmedia storytelling embraces the multiple viewpoints of its various characters.

7. *Performance*. Performance refers to the way transmedia storytelling inspires its audience to contribute to the story (e.g., fan fiction) (Jenkins 2009b).

A good example of transmedia storytelling that embraces all seven principles is the Game of Thrones franchise, centered on George R. R. Martin's Song of Ice and Fire series of novels. The principles can be observed in the franchise's clever use of media during its transmedia marketing campaign that led up to the debut of the first episode of the HBO series, Game of Thrones.

Playing on the five senses, marketing strategist Campfire Media attempted to re-create the experience of living in Westeros through specific sensory clues that represented sound, taste, touch, sight, and smell. Boxes of perfumes were sent to influential bloggers, complete with a map of Westeros. *Spreadability* was demonstrated as those bloggers quickly spread the word. Both *world building* and *immersion* were demonstrated when a virtual world of the Wall was built, which allowed for fans to role-play as Nightwatchers. *Extractability* was demonstrated when food trucks delivered the flavors of Westeros to fans and newcomers in New York and Los Angeles. *Drillability* was demonstrated when the web-based game, *The Maester's Path*, allowed die-hard fans of the books to unlock exclusive content about the HBO series (Bourdaa 2014).

Continuity was demonstrated in the way the transmedia campaign was sustained across physical media—including the sensory clues and food trucks—and web-based media such as the blogosphere and virtual worlds. *Seriality* can be observed in the adaptation of the novels to the television series. *Multiplicity* is demonstrated by the way the narrative has been extended to the HBO series and video games, beyond what takes place in the novels. *Subjectivity* can be observed through the multiple viewpoints of the dozens of characters and supporting characters in the series. Finally, *performance* can be observed in the wikis and fan fiction that have been produced by the enthusiastic fans of the Game of Thrones transmedia franchise.

Transmedia Storytelling Types

While multiple media elements are the hallmark of transmedia storytelling, they may exist as *separate* media outlets that each contribute to a central narrative, or they may exist as a group of media elements that are integrated together into a *single* narrative. For the purpose of discussion, the former will be referred to as multiple-narrative transmedia and the latter will be referred to as single-narrative transmedia (Pratten 2011).

Multiple-Narrative Transmedia

Multiple-narrative transmedia consists of a complex network of distinct and separate story worlds, all circulating around a central narrative, as illustrated in Figure 1.1. Transmedia franchises, like Game of Thrones, are probably the most familiar iteration of multiple-narrative transmedia. However, multiple-narrative transmedia is not limited to Hollywood alone, and any complex storytelling

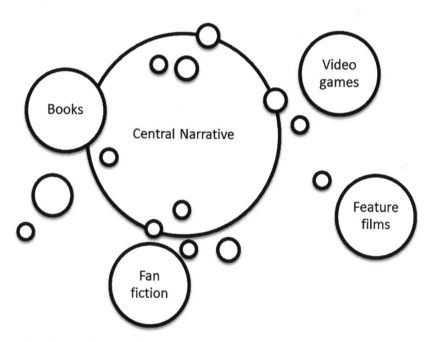

Figure 1.1: Illustration of multiple-narrative transmedia. Multiple story worlds circulating around a central narrative characterize multiple-narrative transmedia storytelling.

project that encompasses multiple, separate storytelling platforms falls into this category. One such example is <u>The Lizzie Bennet Diaries</u> (Kiley, Rorick, and Toole 2012–2014), a multiplatform adaptation of Jane Austen's *Pride and Prejudice*.

Single-Narrative Transmedia

Unlike the multiple storytelling platforms of multiple-narrative transmedia, single-narrative transmedia merges multiple media elements together and delivers them on a single storytelling platform, as illustrated in Figure 1.2. Each media element in single-narrative transmedia is developed as an individual story world that contributes to the overall narrative, but may also be explored on its own merit. In some ways, this type of transmedia storytelling resembles what many would consider to

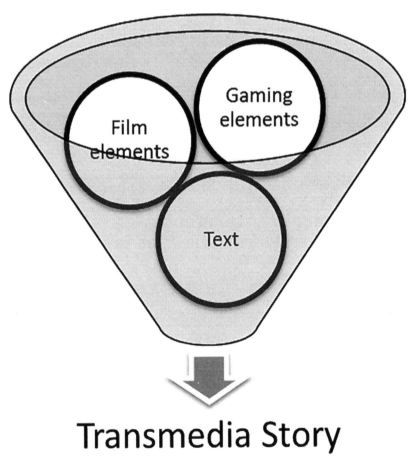

Figure 1.2: Illustration of single-narrative transmedia. Multiple media elements are combined to deliver the narrative on a single storytelling platform.

be digital storytelling. However, digital storytelling would be considered transmedia in nature only if it encompasses features of the seven principles of transmedia storytelling. In that respect, digital storytelling represents a broader category of storytelling of which transmedia storytelling can be considered a subgroup.

Transmedia Storytelling Genres

While single-narrative and multiple-narrative transmedia represent two broad categories of transmedia storytelling, those categories can be further classified into genres. However, unlike the way fiction is classified into genres, transmedia storytelling genres do not reflect themes so much as structure of interactivity—and structure of interactivity is driven by the platforms used to deliver the story. Additionally, some genres of transmedia storytelling may be shaped by the media elements that are used to convey the central narrative.

Single-narrative transmedia, where multiple story worlds are blended together, tends to be formed around a central media element that serves as the primary platform for the narrative. For example, a centrally text-based or audio-based narrative is typical of *interactive fiction*, while a visually centered (e.g., images, animation) narrative is more commonly found in *transmedia games*. Single-narrative transmedia storytelling is usually the work of independent arts groups with small, but very loyal fan bases. By that token, single-narrative transmedia is often of exceptional literary or artistic value.

On the other hand, multiple-narrative transmedia more typically focuses on entertainment value. The *entertainment franchise* is the most common genre for this type of transmedia storytelling, and has been heavily embraced by the movie and gaming industries—and increasingly, the television and publishing industries. Television, movies, and commercial video games serve as the primary delivery platforms in entertainment franchises, taking advantage of big budgets for bigger-than-life productions that attract big fan bases. That being said, smaller productions, such as *transmedia web series*, are a growing genre of multiple-narrative transmedia, made possible by the affordances of the Internet as a direct-to-consumer storytelling delivery vehicle.

The following case studies provide a better picture of what transmedia storytelling looks like. Examples of single-narrative and multiple-narrative transmedia from four genres—transmedia web series, interactive fiction, transmedia games, and transmedia entertainment franchises—are described. All of the productions introduced here appear again in Chapter Five as part of the library programming examples.

Transmedia Web Series

Borrowing elements from television, transmedia web series deliver stories through multiple short web episodes on platforms such as YouTube. Additional narratives are explored through story worlds typically built on social media platforms. The following two case studies represent successful examples of transmedia web series.

The Lizzie Bennet Diaries. The Lizzie Bennet Diaries (Kiley, Rorick, and Toole 2012–2014) is a 2013 Primetime Emmy Award–winning web series that reimagines Jane Austen's *Pride and Prejudice* from the point of view of 24-year-old Lizzie Bennet, a mass communications graduate student who still lives at home with her parents and two sisters. The main story is told in the form of video blogs that Lizzie is producing for her thesis; and they serve as a personal diary, giving viewers a glimpse into her daily social life. Lizzie posts her video blogs to YouTube, and soon becomes an Internet sensation. In true Austen fashion, The Lizzie Bennet Diaries offers a tongue-in-cheek approach to the social problems of the upper class.

In this transmedia project, the world of Lizzie Bennet collides with the real world as the video blogs that Lizzie posts to YouTube make up the actual web series produced by Pemberley Digital. During the airing of the web series, fans could also interact with the characters through story worlds built on the social media platforms Twitter and Tumblr. Though no longer interactive, access to those storytelling platforms is still available through Pemberley Digital's web site (pemberleydigital.com). A book titled *The Secret Diary of Lizzie Bennet* (Su and Rorick 2014) adds another dimension for fans who wish to engage more deeply in the story. The use of transmedia to retell such a classic piece of literature may also serve as a valuable tool for introducing fans to Jane Austen's original works.

Ruby Skye P. I. Ruby Skye P. I. (Golick and Strassman-Cohn 2012–2014) is an award-winning Canadian-based mystery web series geared toward preteens and teens. Ruby is a detective who uses humor and the power of deductive reasoning to solve mysteries in each season of mini-episodes. In season one, *The Spam Scam*, Ruby's neighbor loses her money to an e-mail scam. Ruby enlists the help of her sister Hailey to trace the e-mails back to her school's computers. In season two, *The Haunted Library*, the owner of the library dies suddenly, leaving a mystery behind that requires Ruby to track down Mrs. O'Deary's will. In season three, *The Maltese Puppy*, Ruby investigates the sudden disappearance of donated toys from a local children's charity that mysteriously coincides with the appearance of a Maltese puppy.

The portal of entry into Ruby Skye's world is the Ruby Skye P. I. web site (rubyskyepi.com), which provides access points to all the media platforms that deliver the transmedia storytelling experience. World building is structured through separate media platforms that create multiple points of view and serve as a continuation of the central narrative. For example, fictional web sites for the main characters and the O'Deary Library allow the audience to engage more deeply with the characters in the story. Games that are introduced in the episodes can be played by the audience. In addition, further information on the real-life issues that are woven into the episodes is provided as a takeaway for audience members to use in their daily lives. The integration of real-life issues (e.g., e-mail spam, social issues) into fictional settings makes Ruby Skye P. I. a useful educational tool.

Interactive Fiction

Interactive fiction typically uses text or narration as the focus of the storyline and then builds the story out with additional media elements. This genre of transmedia storytelling is single-narrative, meaning it is delivered through a single platform with each media element in the story serving as a puzzle piece that when put together forms the bigger picture of the story. The following two case studies represent exemplary forms of interactive fiction.

Inanimate Alice. *Inanimate Alice* (Pullinger and Joseph 2005–) is an award–winning transmedia storytelling project that was named a Best Website for Teaching and Learning by the American Association of School Librarians in 2012. Self-described as a "born digital" novel, it blends text with sound, movie, and gaming elements to create an interactive reading experience on screen. The story follows Alice, a globe-trotting girl and budding game designer, through 10 episodes, of which six have been produced. Episode one begins with Alice at the age of eight living in China. By episode three, Alice is 13 years old and is living in Russia. Across all the episodes, readers are invited to play the games Alice creates. Games become increasingly complex in subsequent episodes reflecting Alice's burgeoning skills as a game designer. For example, in episode four, the story and game merge together as one, as readers must help Alice find her way out of an abandoned building.

Each episode of the story is delivered through a single platform, moving from Flash in earlier episodes to Unity in episode five as the gaming elements become more complex. It is the gaming elements that transform *Inanimate Alice* from a multimedia storytelling experience to a truly interactive transmedia storytelling experience that immerses fans in Alice's world, and the story functions very much like a role-playing game. The media elements add layers of depth to the narrative, giving fans subtle clues about Alice's life, and motivating them to engage more deeply with the story. Deep engagement cultivates a deep fan base, of which Alice has many. *Inanimate Alice* has been the inspiration for many fan-created digital stories that reimagine Alice in new story worlds.

Rockford's Rock Opera. *Rockford's Rock Opera* (Sweetapple and Sweetapple 2010) is an award-winning interactive musical audiobook that joins colorful images, animation, sound effects, and songs together to create an immersive storytelling experience. The story is about a boy named Moog and his dog Rockford who end up on the Island of Infinity, a magical place where the last of each animal species goes to live when it becomes extinct. Their adventures lead them to save the Cocklebur Ick, a creature that arrived on the island stuck to the backside of Rockford. Rockford and Moog's quest unfolds over 16 chapters. Themes about ecological awareness run throughout the narrative, which is especially appealing to preschool and elementary-age children.

The story is available on a number of platforms, including web, DVD, and mobile app, though it remains single-narrative because each platform delivers the same story. Individual media elements are pulled out of the story for exploration on the Rockford's Rock Opera web site (rockfordsrockopera.com). Videos, songs, and lyrics, and the read-only text are available for fans to consume separately. Fans can also explore the many characters from the story, along with a map of the Island of Infinity. Additionally, activities from the web site bring fantasy elements into the real world. For example, by making a dog kennel money box, fans can collect money to help Rockford's friends at the Battersea Dogs and Cats Home, which really exists. Fans can also contribute to the narrative by posting pictures of their pets or drawings of extinct creatures to the web site.

Transmedia Games

Transmedia games are sometimes categorized as interactive fiction, and while they do incorporate interactive fictional elements, they can be differentiated by their objectives. That is, the player must meet the goal (i.e., object of the game) in order to complete the story. The following two case studies illustrate the structural features found in transmedia games.

Collapsus. *Collapsus* (Pallotta 2010) is an award-winning transmedia storytelling project that integrates animation, film, and documentary elements into a game that challenges the player to save the planet from an energy crisis. Players are immersed in a story world that follows multiple characters through a global energy crisis. Film and animation alternate with real-life documentary elements that blur the line between fantasy and reality. Players must learn about the causes of the energy crisis—and decide whose point of view to accept as they take on the task to manipulate the world's energy supplies in an effort to prevent a global crisis. The outcome is dependent on the choices the player makes.

Collapsus uses transmedia storytelling to address a global issue in a way that educates players about the multiple perspectives of a real-life problem through fictional characters' points of view. Separate story worlds and storylines are built for each character, giving players the opportunity to engage more deeply with the character of their choice. *Collapsus* is unique in its integration of documentary elements into an otherwise largely fictional narrative space, and the producers cite a declining interest in documentary viewers as the reason for it (Pallotta 2010). Because of its nonfiction elements, there is strong potential for the project to be used as an educational tool.

Gone Home. *Gone Home* (The Fullbright Company 2013) is an award-winning story exploration game that uses music, audio narration, books, journal entries, and art to create an interactive world where the player looks for clues in an empty house, trying to piece them together to discover the story's plot. The game begins as 21-year-old Kaitlin arrives home from a year abroad and finds a note from her sister, Samantha, tacked to the front door of her house telling her to not go "digging around to find out where I am." The player takes on the role of Kaitlin in exploring each room of the house to gather the kinds of details needed to unveil the plot.

Gone Home is a fully interactive and immersive transmedia experience, delivering the story in the form of clues scattered throughout the house, making the object of the game one of story making. The game is unique in the way the principles of transmedia storytelling are handled. For example, the clues represent the characters in the story, requiring the player to find and interpret multiple points of view rather than receive them through the storytelling process. Also, although the game is single-narrative, multiple retellings of the story are possible because no two players explore the house in exactly the same way. Finally, the lack of action in the game serves as a motivating factor for action by players to dig more deeply to find the details that tell the story of Kaitlin's family. Its unique format has had a polarizing effect on the gaming world, with some questioning whether or not to even consider it a game. However, among educators, *Gone Home* has garnered interest as a tool for developing critical literacy skills and as a possible alternative to text-based stories (Sung 2015).

Transmedia Entertainment Franchises

Jenkins's concept of transmedia storytelling is based on his observations of the television, film, and gaming industries where transmedia entertainment franchises originated. The abundant resources of those industries make the production of transmedia entertainment feasible. The two case studies that follow were chosen as representative models of how the sheer spreadability of transmedia franchises creates multiple narratives that can be used for both entertainment and educational purposes.

PBS KIDS Transmedia. PBS KIDS Transmedia is part of PBS's Ready To Learn program that focuses on early literacy and math skills development. The Ready To Learn program was developed as a partnership between Congress, the U.S. Department of Education, PBS, the Corporation for Public Broadcasting, and local public stations with the goal of targeting at-risk kids. The program has taken PBS's most popular children's television shows and expanded them to online videos, games, and printable activities that are accessible from the PBS KIDS web site (pbskids.org). Many of the stories in the PBS KIDS franchise are preexisting children's literature, including Dr. Seuss's *The Cat in the Hat*, H. A. Rey's *Curious George*, and Susan Meddaugh's *Martha Speaks*.

The PBS KIDS children's television shows function as the primary entry point into the transmedia franchise. As children (and their parents) become fans of the characters, they are motivated to further explore the PBS KIDS web site to experience the stories in new and educational ways. Even deeper exploration of the stories takes place through the stories' books—some of which are part of the PBS KIDS franchise and others that predate it. Finally, in true transmedia franchise style, children's merchandise (e.g., t-shirts, dolls) rounds out the storytelling experience. While PBS's use of transmedia does serve as entertainment for children, it goes beyond that through its educational objectives. A key finding from research on the Ready To Learn program found "that when TV shows and electronic resources have been carefully designed to incorporate what is known about effective reading instruction, they serve as positive and powerful tools for teaching and learning" (Corporation of Public Broadcasting 2011).

Star Wars. Star Wars is one of the earliest examples of transmedia entertainment, and considered by many to be a benchmark for transmedia entertainment franchises. Starting with the original trilogy of movies in the late 1970s and early 1980s, the Star Wars franchise spans decades with storylines that encompass seven feature films, as well as comic books, novels, an animated television series, video games, and merchandise (*Wookieepedia: The Star Wars Wiki* 2015). Fans have contributed prolifically to the franchise through fan-created fiction and films. The Disney parks' *Star Tours—The Adventure Continues* takes the transmedia experience to a whole new level by fully immersing fans in the story world through 3-D simulated space flights that feature the characters and settings of both the original and prequel film trilogies (Walt Disney World n.d.). The Star Wars transmedia entertainment franchise has gone far beyond world building to create an entire universe, and they even have a name for it—the Expanded Universe (*Wookieepedia: The Star Wars Wiki* 2015).

Conclusion

Transmedia storytelling is a new form of storytelling where fictional story worlds are built and delivered across multiple media platforms to create an immersive and interactive narrative universe that blurs the lines between fantasy and reality. Transmedia storytelling fosters deep engagement in the storyline, creating a strong audience base that is motivated to participate in the storytelling process through fan-created works. The convergence of fictional story worlds and storytelling technologies makes transmedia storytelling an exceptional resource for 21st-century libraries.

CHAPTER 2

Making Literacy Connections

Multimodality ▪ New Literacies ▪ New Media Literacies ▪ The Play-Literacy Connection ▪ A New Way of Reading

The multiple media platforms that are fundamental to transmedia storytelling require participants in the transmedia experience to practice the types of technology-driven literacies most commonly referred to as *digital literacy, media literacy, visual literacy, information literacy,* or *multimodal literacy.* These literacies represent the understanding that literacy is a social practice that is situated within cultural contexts, and meaning-making is uniquely expressed through different cultures' art, language, music, movement, and so on (Harster 2003). The literacy practices that are connected to transmedia storytelling find roots in the theory of multimodality, breadth in the theory of New Literacies, and action in the skills of the new media literacies. The elements of storytelling and gameplay embody these literacy practices that together, forge a new way of reading.

Multimodality

Multimodality is the theoretical framework by which literacy has been reconceptualized to explain how new modes of communication impact language and writing. A mode is a tool that is used for the purpose of meaning-making or communication. Kress (2010) referred to multimodality as a *theory of semiotics* (i.e., signs) rather than linguistics (i.e., language), thus expanding meaning-making beyond language and text to include images, sounds, 3-D objects, color, and more. Multimodality is foundational to an understanding of the multiple literacies of transmedia storytelling, and the four features of multimodal theory help define it: materiality (of mode), framing, design, and production.

Materiality refers to the materials and properties that make up a mode and that impact the mode's capabilities to express meaning or convey a message. Social, cultural, historical, and institutional influences shape the materiality of a mode. Social media tools are examples of modes that are used for communication. Still, among the various social media modes, differences exist in materiality, which impact the way they are used to communicate messages. This is illustrated in a case study of a transmedia storytelling experiment called TravelPlot Porto, where tourists in Porto, Portugal, were invited to take part in a treasure hunt or follow it on social media (Twitter, Pinterest, and YouTube) through the eyes of Peter, a fictional character. During the 12-week event, Twitter engagement was average, Pinterest gained the greatest following, and YouTube had the lowest engagement. Pinterest's popularity in the experiment was most likely due to its materiality as a visually graphic tool with discovery browsing capabilities—the images of Porto and Portugal appeared to be pinned across multiple boards, creating a promotional impact for the city (Ferreiraa, Alvesa, and Quicob 2014).

Framing refers to the way in which elements are connected or stand apart in a mode in order to signify meaning (Kress 2010). For example, each sentence in this book is a frame, and the means used to convey the message that "this is a sentence" are punctuation marks (i.e., commas, periods, semicolons). The means we use to frame modes are specific to that mode—punctuation in sentences, rising and falling action in a story, codas in music, running credits that signify the end of a movie, and so on. In other words, frames function as culturally shaped concepts that facilitate interpretation, or as Wolf (2006) describes, "basic orientational aids that help us navigate through our experiential universe" (5). The concept of frames has implications for transmedia storytelling because frames themselves can be considered transmedial. Saldre and Torop (2012) use the example of *Pottermore*, a virtual world based on the Harry Potter series, to illustrate this. Fans experience the wizarding world through the frame of role-play in *Pottermore*. This differs from the means by which the novels or the films frame it. Yet, all three platforms

> " The design elements in *Pottermore* allude to the full-scale wizarding world of Harry Potter, creating a sense of intermediality between the virtual world and the original story. "

provide fans with a continuity of experience in the wizarding world, illustrating the transmedia nature of framing.

Design refers to the placement of elements in a given mode and is used to shape interpretation of informational value (Jewitt 2006). For example, the use of headings, tables, and figures in this book provides readers with information about the subjects covered in each chapter. The design of such elements is based on standards and expectations given by the publisher.

Design is conceptual rather than concrete, but the usability of a mode can be dependent on it. Imagine how the usability of this book would be impacted if there were no headings or figures at all (it would be difficult to read to say the least). Transmedia storytelling is particularly dependent on design because good design creates an immersive experience across multiple storytelling platforms. The key design feature inherent in transmedia storytelling is intermediality, defined as the many ways in which transmedia content makes "intertextual references through linking, allusion, recombination, extension, association, fusion, hybridisation, adaptation, translation, or synthesis" (Davis 2013, 176) to the central narrative. In other words, intermediality can be thought of as the transmedial framing that occurs across multiple media platforms, as discussed in the *Pottermore* example previously.

Production refers to the creative process that results in the output of an actual product (i.e., book, movie, website, play) (Sanders and Albers 2010). The creative process includes all the skills (e.g., technical skills, critical thinking, collaboration) used to make the product. Product creation is influenced by the creator's cultural and social experiences with other products (Doloughan 2011). For example, in an interview with the American Film Institute (Spielberg 2012), director Steven Spielberg discussed the important influence of the classic film *Lawrence of Arabia* on his movie making. Yet, Spielberg's own artistic influence transcends the film industry as evidenced in his inclusion in *Time* magazine's top 100 influential people in the world (Brokaw 2013). For transmedia storytelling, production takes on a double meaning. While transmedia content is most certainly the product of a creative team, the participatory culture that transmedia storytelling feeds inspires and influences the audience to contribute to the narrative, thus turning the audience into creators or producers as well.

Multimodal theory has been pivotal in forming a new perspective of literacy as a set of social and cultural practices. Two conceptual understandings of literacy based on multimodal theory—the new literacies and the new media literacies—are particularly well suited to the discussion of transmedia storytelling.

New Literacies

The concept of *new literacies* has different meanings depending upon the field or disciplinary perspective from which it is used: new literacies as social practices (Street 1995), multiliteracies (New London Group 1996), literacies of online comprehension (Coiro 2003), literacies as social discourses (Gee 2007a), multimodal literacies (Sanders and Albers 2010), and new literacies as a construct of other disciplinary perspectives (Lankshear and Knobel 2006; Leu et al. 2013). When specific terms are used to describe literacy, such as digital literacy, information literacy, media literacy, or visual literacy, the net of new literacies gets even bigger. Aligning transmedia storytelling to literacy requires an examination of a broad range of literacies, so for that reason, the concept of new literacies (Lankshear and Knobel 2006; Leu et al. 2013) as a construct is explored in this section.

Literacy and technology expert Donald Leu first proposed a construct to define new literacies in the 2002 edition of *What Research Has to Say about Reading Instruction*. His proposal grew from the observation that an ever-changing set of literacies would be needed to keep up with the fast-paced growth of innovations in information and communication technologies. These new literacies, primarily driven by Internet-based technologies, would require new ways of reading and writing in addition to traditional print-based notions of literacy. In that way, the new literacies did not replace traditional literacy, but extended it.

Leu's (2002) earlier conceptualization of new literacies was further developed into a working theory of New Literacies. The theory is dual-level, framing the new literacies into lowercase (new literacies) and uppercase (New Literacies). The uppercase theory focuses on unifying the concept of New Literacies across a wide range of disciplines, while lowercase theories focus on specific disciplinary perspectives of the new literacies.

Uppercase Theory of New Literacies

Leu et al. (2013) proposed a set of central principles that they identified as common denominators found within current research activities across the various disciplines that make up New Literacies. The principles defining the uppercase theory of New Literacies are as follows:

> 66 The New Literacies (uppercase for emphasis) is an umbrella term that describes the commonalities of all the new literacies collectively. 99

1. Contemporary notions of literacy are defined by Internet-related technologies.

2. New Literacies are required to fully utilize the affordances of Internet-related technologies.

3. The New Literacies are deictic (i.e., situated and contextual).

4. The New Literacies are socially constructed practices.

5. The New Literacies are multimodal.

6. The New Literacies require different strategies for meaning-making.

7. The New Literacies demand greater critical literacies.

8. The New Literacies are more complex than traditional literacies, both changing the educator's role and making it more important than ever (Leu et al. 2013).

The principles of New Literacies share commonalities with the principles of transmedia storytelling, demonstrating the strong literacy connections that transmedia storytelling can make with its audience. Table 2.1 aligns the seven principles of transmedia storytelling with the principles of the uppercase theory of New Literacies.

Arguably, transmedia storytelling, like the New Literacies, would not exist in its current state without the benefit of Internet technologies such as e-mail, social media, and web streaming. Each story world that makes up a transmedia storytelling universe is also deictic, illustrating the multimodality inherent in the New Literacies. That is, each media platform that represents a story world situates the characters and storyline within a specific context in order to explore and expand the transmedia storytelling universe, creating a multimodal storytelling experience. Like the New Literacies, transmedia storytelling is also very much a socially constructed practice, and the participatory culture that results from a transmedia story's strong fan base is an example of how the audience socially constructs its own story world. In other words, the creation and interpretation of transmedia storytelling is a social practice reflected within the principles of the New Literacies.

Lowercase Theories of new literacies

Lowercase theories study individual areas of the new literacies that serve to inform the broader theory of New Literacies. Literacies such as digital literacy, information literacy, media literacy, and

> 66 The new literacies (lowercase emphasis) refer to individual literacies that are being studied across different disciplines (e.g., information literacy, digital literacy). 99

Table 2.1: Aligning Transmedia Storytelling with the New Literacies

Principles of Transmedia Storytelling	Principles of the New Literacies	Literacy Connections
Spreadability vs. Drillability	New Literacies are required to fully utilize the affordances of Internet-related technologies.	Ease of spreadability exists because of the affordances of Internet-related technologies (e.g., social media).
	New Literacies require different strategies for meaning-making.	Different strategies for meaning-making are needed for deep engagement, or drillability.
Continuity vs. Multiplicity	New Literacies are multimodal.	Multimodality is a central characteristic of transmedia storytelling, allowing for both continuity and multiplicity across multiple media platforms.
Immersion vs. Extractability	New Literacies are deictic.	Fans become immersed within the deictic center of the story world, and then extract elements of the story to use within the contexts of their real lives.
World Building	New Literacies are deictic.	World building is a deictic process, and all story worlds are situated within the context of the characters and plot.
Seriality	New Literacies are multimodal.	Multimodality allows for seriality to take place across multiple media outlets.
Subjectivity	New Literacies demand greater critical literacies.	Critical literacies are essential for comprehending the multiple viewpoints (i.e., subjectivity) of characters within their story worlds.
Performance	New Literacies are socially constructed practices.	Fan fiction (i.e., performance) is an example of how the audience socially constructs new practices in retellings of the story.

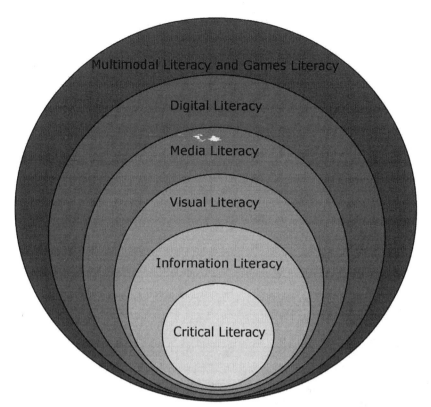

Figure 2.1: The seven literacies of transmedia storytelling. This figure shows the multi-layered relationships between the literacy practices of transmedia storytelling. At the core lies critical literacy, indicating its central importance as a function of all the new literacies.

so forth fall into the lowercase level of new literacies. There are seven lowercase literacies that form the literacy structure of transmedia storytelling—critical literacy, information literacy, visual literacy, media literacy, digital literacy, games literacy, and multimodal literacy. Figure 2.1 illustrates the relationship between them.

Critical literacy requires consumers of texts to actively participate in the reading process, essentially "destructuring" and "restructuring" a text in order to develop a critical understanding of its social context, meaning, and purpose (McLaughlin and DeVoogd 2004; Lankshear 1997). Transmedia storytelling requires critical literacy skills in the "destructuring" and "restructuring" of multiple modes of text, positioning it at the core of transmedia storytelling and illustrating its importance within all areas of the new literacies.

Information literacy is the ability to "recognize when information is needed and have the ability to locate, evaluate, and use effectively the needed information" (American Library Association 1989, para. 3).

Information literacy is situated just above critical literacy in the "seven literacies" figure because it is transmedial, meaning it can be applied across all modes of transmedia storytelling—physical (e.g., books) and virtual (e.g., films). Furthermore, the interactivity and immersive values of transmedia storytelling require the use of information literacy skills to navigate story worlds and synthesize multiple modes of information in order to successfully participate in the transmedia experience.

Visual literacy is the ability to read, write, and solve problems with visual information and enhances other forms of literacy (Baker 2012). Like information literacy, visual literacy is transmedial in its ability to be applied to all visual information across all modes of transmedia storytelling, whether print, digital, or animated. Because visual literacy can also be thought of as visual *information literacy*, it was placed directly above information literacy in the figure.

Media literacy is defined as "the ability to access, analyze, evaluate, and communicate information in a variety of forms" (NAMLE 2015, para. 1) and is also transmedial in nature, encompassing both print and digital information. Media literacy is closely related to visual literacy, and is sometimes used interchangeably with information literacy. In the "seven literacies" figure, media literacy is situated above both visual and information literacy to illustrate its encircling relationship. Because transmedia storytelling exists across multiple forms of media, media literacy must be exercised to evaluate the messages from each media platform before holistic meaning-making can take place. When fans contribute to the transmedia narrative, they are exercising the communication component of media literacy.

In an interview in *Educational Leadership* (Pool 1997), Paul Gilster defined digital literacy as "the ability to understand information and—more important—to evaluate and integrate information in multiple formats that the computer can deliver" (6). In that sense, digital literacy can be viewed as the application of information, visual and media literacy skills to digital technologies, therefore situating its place in the "seven literacies" illustrated in Figure 2.1 as a circle encompassing media, visual, and information literacies. Digital technologies are centrally important to the spreadability, multiplicity, seriality, and performance principles of transmedia storytelling, making digital literacy skills essential for both comprehension of and contribution to the transmedia storytelling experience.

Games literacy and multimodal literacy are interrelated. Games literacy is defined as "developing expertise in designing rewarding experiences for oneself within a game world (particularly within the game's semiotic and rule systems)" (Squire 2008, 640). Games literacy might be viewed as the joint application of digital, media, visual, information, and critical literacy skills, essentially making games literacy a multimodal literacy—which is defined as the "integration of multiple modes of communication and expression" (NCTE 2008, para. 1) for transformative meaning-making. To become an expert at gameplay requires critical discrimination of the game environment (i.e., multimodal meaning-making), strategic thinking about game moves (i.e., digital literacy), and accurate application of game rules (i.e., information literacy). Games literacy was included along with multimodal literacy as the outer circle of Figure 2.1 because of its prominent importance in transmedia storytelling.

The structure of new literacies that transmedia storytelling is comprised of makes it a powerful literacy tool. In fact, transmedia storytelling may in itself represent a new kind of literacy practice altogether—transmedia literacy. The concept of transmedia literacy takes us back to media studies scholar Henry Jenkins. Building on the concept of new literacies, Jenkins (2009a) identified a set of skills referred to as new media literacies that he believes are necessary for participating in a new media culture. The new media literacies incorporate transmedia-related skills and are discussed in the next section.

New Media Literacies

Jenkins (2009a) describes the new media literacies as "a set of cultural competencies and social skills that young people need in the new media landscape" (xiii). In that respect, the new media literacies fit into the paradigm of lowercase literacies in the framework of New Literacies theory. Jenkins defines new media literacies in the context of specific skill sets that learners need in order to actively participate in a digital culture. These skill sets are the same skills needed for interacting with transmedia storytelling, making transmedia storytelling an important tool for developing the new media literacies.

Eleven skills make up the new media literacies (Jenkins 2009a), altogether painting a picture of what a participatory culture looks like—a participatory culture in which transmedia storytelling serves a large part. The first skill in the new media literacies is *play*, a form of experimentation and problem solving. Play is central to the transmedia storytelling experience and is most obviously noticeable within transmedia storytelling's gaming elements. The second

> " The experience of fully engaging in the transmedia storytelling experience exercises the 11 skills that make up the new media literacies. "

skill is *performance*, which is the ability to role-play and improvise as a function of discovery and learning. Performance is also one of the seven principles of transmedia storytelling, which occurs when the audience contributes to the story (e.g., fan fiction). The third skill in the new media literacies is *simulation*, which is the ability to understand and build models of real-life processes. Simulation is similar to the principle of world building in transmedia storytelling, where the story world is built to intersect with the audience's daily life. The fourth skill is *appropriation*, which is the ability to remix media content to create something new. Appropriation is similar to the principle of multiplicity in transmedia storytelling, where the story gets retold in new ways rather than merely adapted to a new medium.

The fifth skill in the new media literacies is *multitasking*, which is the ability to change one's focus as needed toward the most important details in the environment. Multitasking is a skill for transmedia storytelling for the purpose of identifying and focusing on the common elements of each storytelling platform to make sense of the whole transmedia universe. The sixth skill is *distributed cognition*, which is the ability to "interact meaningfully with tools that expand mental capacities." Distributed cognition is necessary as a skill of multimodality, also inherent in transmedia storytelling. The seventh skill in the new media literacies is *collective intelligence*, which is the ability to take part in groupthink in order to meet a commonly shared goal. Collective intelligence is central to the culture of fan-based contributions in transmedia storytelling. The eighth skill is *judgment*, which is the ability to evaluate the credibility of information. In transmedia storytelling, the lines between fantasy and reality sometimes blur (see the *Collapsus* case study in Chapter One as an example), requiring the use of judgment to discern fact from fiction.

The ninth skill in the new media literacies is *transmedia navigation*, which is the ability to track the trajectory of information across multiple media platforms, as in transmedia storytelling. The 10th skill is *networking*, which is the ability to find, synthesize, and share information. Networking is a fundamental function of the participatory culture of transmedia storytelling. For example, *Wookieepedia: The Star Wars Wiki* (2015) demonstrates the power of networking as it is considered a primary source for anything and everything Star Wars–related. The 11th and final skill in the new media literacies is *negotiation*, which is the ability to recognize and respect multiple points of view. Negotiation is similar to the principle of subjectivity in transmedia storytelling, which embraces the multiple viewpoints of its various characters.

While the new media literacies are integrally connected to transmedia storytelling, they are also reflective of the types of 21st-century skills (e.g., critical thinking, collaboration, communication, creativity) that have been identified by organizations such as the Partnership for 21st Century Learning and the American Association of School Librarians—skills that should be familiar to most educators. The connection between the new media literacies and 21st-century learning further highlights the emerging importance of transmedia storytelling as a tool that promotes the contemporary understandings of literacy as a set of social and cultural practices.

The Play-Literacy Connection

Perhaps the greatest of all the literacy affordances that transmedia storytelling has to offer is that of play, one of the skill sets of the new media literacies. Play is known to be one of the earliest avenues for literacy development (Roskos and Christie 2001), but is often discussed in terms of traditional print-based literacy, though play itself is most certainly a multimodal literacy (NCTE 2008). Play is inherent in transmedia storytelling through two very important components—storytelling and gameplay—which together can be thought of as transmedia play.

Storytelling as Play-Based Literacy

Children naturally exhibit their storytelling abilities through the course of pretend play. Everyday objects become something new, the roles of others are played out, and dolls and puppets are given voices in elaborate scenarios (The Child Development Institute 2013). These are the informal ways in which children practice storytelling through play.

Wohlwend (2008) described play as a "literacy of possibilities" (127). In doing so, she introduced the concept of play as a multimodal literacy practice. Storytelling within the context of play can then be viewed as both multimodal and transmedial. In other words, when children create stories that continue across the multiple modes of pretend play (e.g., props, songs, art, physical movement), they are practicing transmedia storytelling, albeit informally.

Cassell and Ryokai (2001) suggested that technology can serve an important role in fostering children's storytelling play. They introduced the StoryMat, a soft play mat that had the capability of recording and playing back children's stories during pretend play. The system was used as a collaborative storytelling tool that allowed a given child to hear other children's recorded narratives during play on the mat. In listening to others' stories, the child was encouraged to continue the themes of the storyline through a new story. In a small study of 36 children between the ages of 5 and 8 that used the StoryMat, findings indicated that the collaborative affordances of the system sometimes prompted children to take on the role of a central narrator, summarizing the story for the listener, or direct other children's narrative creations in a collaborative storytelling process—both examples of developmentally advanced narratives.

Storytelling is a multimodal literacy practice that can be seen in its earliest form in the pretend play of young children. Collaborative storytelling, as in the StoryMat case, demonstrates how a participatory culture is relevant to even the earliest stages of literacy development. The success of the StoryMat experiment in prompting developmentally advanced narratives in young children during storytelling play has implications for how transmedia storytelling as a collaborative tool might do the same for other age groups.

Gameplay as Literacy

Gameplay—whether through full-length transmedia games, minigames within a transmedia story, or gaming elements (gamification)—is central to the interactive and immersive qualities of transmedia storytelling. Gee (2007b) suggests that the process of becoming proficient at playing digital games is the process of practicing a new literacy—games literacy to be precise. Games literacy is a multimodal literacy, and one of the seven literacies of transmedia storytelling. It requires multimedia navigation and creation, as well as analyzing and synthesizing information from multiple modes or formats (NCTE 2008).

Steinkuehler (2010) sees games as a "digital literacy practice through and through" (61). She argues that both reading and writing take place within a digital game. Players must read a game's meanings, and then respond by writing back into the game. The concept of reading and writing in games reflects a semiotic understanding of literacy in the same way that it does for transmedia storytelling—both share roots in the theoretical framework of multimodality. Players not only read words but also read sounds and images in order to learn how to play the game; and those words, sounds, and images are situated specifically within the context of the game's domain (Gee 2007b).

> 66 Online reading comprehension demands multiple forms of literacy, encompassing the seven literacies of transmedia storytelling. 99

Avid gamers belong to a community of practice and become experts in gaming through participation in the practices surrounding the gaming culture. In the same way, fans of a transmedia universe become experts in world building when contributing their own creations to the transmedia storytelling experience. Therefore, gameplay, when enhanced by the immersive nature of transmedia storytelling, promotes a truly participatory culture that goes beyond games literacy to promote multimodal literacy—or perhaps more fittingly, transmedia literacy.

A New Way of Reading

The rich narratives so characteristic of transmedia storytelling offer a new way of experiencing reading that simultaneously supports the literacies of *online reading comprehension*. While sharing some of the same skills as traditional reading comprehension, online reading comprehension requires additional skills. Leu et al. (2015) described a number of literacy practices that define the process of online reading comprehension. Successful online reading comprehension requires the ability to:

1. *Identify* important questions when reading online.
2. *Locate* and *Evaluate* the quality and validity of information in online environments.

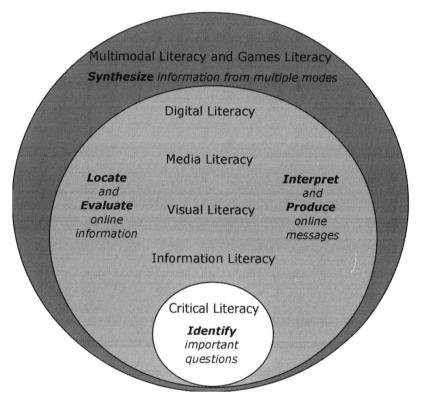

Figure 2.2: Online reading comprehension as a function of the seven literacies of transmedia storytelling. With critical literacy at its core, the seven literacies of transmedia storytelling are exercised during the practice of reading a transmedia story, making transmedia storytelling an ideal tool for the development of online reading comprehension.

3. *Synthesize* information from multiple modes in online environments.

4. *Interpret* and *Produce* messages to communicate in online environments.

The actions required for reading across the multiple modes of texts that make up transmedia storytelling—both print and online texts—are not only demanding of the skills of online reading comprehension but also frequently require those of traditional reading comprehension as well. Figure 2.2 illustrates the skills of online reading comprehension, which reflect the seven literacies of transmedia storytelling (as seen in Figure 2.1), making transmedia storytelling an excellent source for librarians to promote and support the development of online reading comprehension, and more broadly, 21st-century learning.

Reading to define important questions might mean identifying the information needed to interact with the transmedia story—a critical literacy in both print and digital domains. Locating information might mean uncovering all the entry points into the storytelling universe. Evaluating information might mean deciding the most useful strategies for navigation across multiple story worlds. Both locating and evaluating information are central skills for information literacy, but also relatedly for visual, media, and digital literacies.

Producing online messages—often recognized as media literacy, but also inherent in digital, information, and visual literacies—might mean participating in an online fan forum, or it might mean contributing to a transmedia story through the creation of a new story world (e.g., fan fiction). Synthesizing information from multiple modes might mean putting clues together to solve problems in a game; or it might mean following storylines across multiple modes in order to gain a meta-comprehension of the transmedia storytelling universe—reflecting both games and multimodal literacies. Taken altogether, the skills of online reading comprehension reflect Jenkins's description of transmedia navigation as a new approach to reading within the transmedia storytelling experience (Herr-Stephenson et al. 2013).

Conclusion

Transmedia storytelling is so rich in literacy connections—from multimodality to the New Literacies to the new media literacies—that it has the potential to serve as a powerful literacy tool that supports the development of the kinds of skills that 21st-century learners need. The promise of play (i.e., transmedia play) makes transmedia storytelling a particularly attractive tool for librarians to use in the pursuit of promoting and supporting the literacy development of library users. It is these characteristics that make transmedia storytelling an essential resource for libraries whose missions are to support 21st-century literacies and lifelong learning.

CHAPTER 3

Learning through Transmedia Play

Five Characteristics of Transmedia Play ■ **Learning through Storytelling**
■ **Learning through Gameplay** ■ **Transmedia Storytelling as Gameplay**
■ **Transmedia Storytelling as a Learning Tool**

Transmedia play can be thought of as the practice of reading across multiple platforms in order to engage in transmedia storytelling. This innovative approach to reading creates connections between reading and learning in print, and reading and learning in digital formats (e.g., transmedia navigation), tied together by the critical literacies of traditional and online reading comprehension as discussed in Chapter Two. Two elements in particular make transmedia play a narrative-rich experience: storytelling and gameplay. Both storytelling and gameplay have been found to be beneficial learning tools in and of themselves, but when combined, create a remarkably valuable tool for supporting learning and literacy. The multimodality and participatory nature of transmedia storytelling make transmedia play a capable tool for embracing all aspects of 21st-century learning: critical thinking, collaboration, communication, and creativity.

Five Characteristics of Transmedia Play

Alper and Herr-Stephenson (2013) proposed the idea of transmedia play as a way of supporting children's development of the skills of the new media literacies. They believe that five characteristics make transmedia storytelling a valuable tool for literacy development:

1. Resourcefulness
2. Sociality
3. Mobility
4. Accessibility
5. Replayability

Resourcefulness is creative problem solving using a diversity of sources. For example, the <u>Skeleton Creek</u> series by Patrick Carman uses books and videos to deliver the story in a two-part format. A Skeleton Creek Is Real web site (skeletoncreekisreal.com) and a Skeleton Creek Investigations Facebook page add intrigue to the transmedia experience. Readers must use resourcefulness when following the storyline across multiple platforms in order to solve the mystery.

Sociality reflects the physical and virtual networking that is intrinsic to the participatory culture of transmedia storytelling. For example, *Pottermore* allows Harry Potter fans to connect and socialize with each other in a virtual world; and Harry Potter conventions and festivals are held on an ongoing basis so that fans may meet up in physical spaces. Libraries can support the sociality aspect of transmedia storytelling by providing the access and space for both virtual and physical meet-ups to take place among a particular story's fans.

Mobility refers to the mobile technologies used in transmedia storytelling, and also to the mobile movement of characters and storylines across multiple media platforms. For example, mobility can be seen with the transmedia project, *Robot Heart Stories* (Weiler 2011). *Robot Heart Stories* was an educational experiment that enabled students from two classrooms—one in Montreal and one in Los Angeles—to follow the story of a robot that crash landed in Montreal. The students were given the mission to use math, science, social studies, and creative writing skills to help the robot make her way to Los Angeles to get to her spaceship. As progress was made, new pictures were posted of the robot in various physical locations along the route home.

Accessibility refers to the multiple entry points that exist for experiencing transmedia storytelling. For example, PBS KIDS' Ready To Learn program uses multiple entry points for children to experience their favorite characters from PBS children's television. The goal of this transmedia franchise is to support early literacy and math development, particularly in the at-risk population. Research indicates that the Ready To Learn program is positively impacting the development of those skills (Corporation of Public Broadcasting 2011).

Replayability refers to the high level of detail and intricacy in transmedia storytelling that motivates participants to revisit the story over and over again to gain new perspectives and understandings. For example, *Inanimate Alice* (Pullinger and Joseph 2005–) requires readers to revisit each episode a number of times to fully gain understanding of the multiple layers of meaning that each media element brings to the story. In fact, the storytelling project has been used in language arts classrooms as a multimodal tool that supports the development of close reading skills (Hovious 2014).

Learning through Storytelling

Storytelling is an ancient teaching and learning tool, perhaps as old as language itself. Before the advent of the written word, storytelling was the only tool available for preserving custom, culture, and history. Today, storytelling is still used as an informal pedagogical tool that enhances the conceptualization of concepts, enabling learners to connect prior knowledge to new learning, thus making cognitive processing more meaningful and more memorable (Abrahamson 1998). Storytelling has also made its way into more formal curricular and pedagogical practices.

The Storytelling Curriculum

Storytelling has long been used as a tool for literacy development in young children. Librarians know this very well, as story times are as traditional a part of library services as lending books. Pedagogically speaking, storytelling belongs in the category of play-based curricula, and perhaps the most well-known curriculum of this type is Vivian Gussin Paley's (1990) two-part storytelling curriculum consisting of dictation and dramatization, where children first dictate a story to the teacher, followed by dramatization or acting out of the story by the class.

For Paley, the use of dramatic play as a part of storytelling is key to children's language and narrative development. Cooper (2005) analyzed Paley's storytelling curriculum through the lens of balanced literacy, a widely used approach to teaching reading that strives to utilize the best elements from both whole language and phonics. The balanced literacy approach is generally described as being composed of five

> " The participatory culture of transmedia storytelling is an ideal fit for Paley's storytelling curriculum. "

components: the read aloud, guided reading, shared reading, independent reading, and word study (Parr and Campbell 2012); and Cooper (2005) identified six areas of development within the balanced literacy approach that the storytelling curriculum potentially benefits:

1. *Oral language development.* Dictating stories allows children to contribute to the storytelling process, motivating them to think, imagine, and speak. Dramatization further develops oral language through the delivery of dialogue.

2. *Narrative development.* Dictating stories teaches children how narratives work. Dramatization is the physical construction of narrative.

3. *Conventions of print.* As dictated stories are written down, children observe the process of story writing in action, giving them insights into conventions of print that go beyond the print in books. Dramatization reinforces awareness of a written story or script.

4. *Encoding and decoding.* As dictated stories are written down, children begin to recognize the concept of encoding (writing) and decoding (comprehending).

5. *Word study.* As dictated stories are written down, children are able to see the words that they are speaking and begin to make connections between letters and sounds.

6. *Reading comprehension.* Telling stories through dictation enhances comprehension or meaning-making, much in the same way that writing enhances reading comprehension. Dramatization facilitates meaning-making as children act out the written story.

Paley's storytelling curriculum has much in common with the participatory culture of transmedia storytelling. In both cases, participants—whether the young children that Paley observed or the fans that Jenkins observed—participate in the storytelling process through contribution (i.e., dictating or writing) and interactivity (i.e., acting out or role-play). Cooper established how Paley's storytelling curriculum can fit within the widely used balanced literacy approach. Her analysis has implications for transmedia storytelling, and one need look no further than PBS KIDS' Ready To Learn program (see Chapter One for case study) as an example of the promising benefits of transmedia storytelling for early literacy development.

> "Critical pedagogy combined with place-based education can be thought of as critical storytelling pedagogy. The affordances of transmedia storytelling make it well suited for such a pedagogy."

Critical Storytelling Pedagogy

Critical pedagogy emerged from a philosophical movement that held the belief that all education is politically motivated and therefore oppressive (Freire 1985, 2000). To combat oppression, the movement emphasized pedagogical practices that promote and support critical thinking about social differences, focusing on voice and agency in the classroom, active citizenship, engagement with real-life issues, and social transformation (Kalantzis and Cope 2012). Though critical pedagogy is almost always associated with urban contexts, Gruenewald (2003) suggested that place-based education—typically associated with experiential learning in rural and ecological contexts—is a mirror image of critical pedagogy. He proposed critical pedagogy of place as a convergence of the two pedagogies.

Both critical pedagogy and place-based education have ties to storytelling through what might be considered a critical storytelling pedagogy. Critical storytelling pedagogy, or counter-storytelling (Solorzano and Yasso 2002), focuses on learners' life experiences within a social, cultural, and historical context with the objective to tell the stories of groups that may normally be marginalized within society. While advances in technology continually create new media through which counter-storytelling can be told (e.g., digital storytelling), a participatory culture creates new *medialities* (ways and means) in which counter-storytelling can take place. In that respect, the concept of transmedia storytelling represents a new mediality for counter-storytelling rather than a new medium. Principles of transmedia storytelling, such as subjectivity (multiple view points) and spreadability (ease of circulation) make counter-storytelling within this mediality particularly potent for giving a voice to the marginalized.

Learning through Gameplay

According to the Entertainment Software Association (2015), 155 million Americans play digital games and four out of five U.S. households own a device that can be used to play games. Digital gaming is now a ubiquitous part of society and a phenomenon that has led researchers to explore the impact of digital games on learning. Digital game–based learning (DGBL) research aims to connect the design of successful gaming environments with the design

> 66 Transmedia storytelling encompasses the features of good digital games, making transmedia stories ideal tools for promoting 21st-century learning and literacies. 99

of successful learning environments (Rieber 1996; Shute, Rieber, and Van Eck 2012). Transmedia storytelling has been identified as a subcategory of DGBL (Raybourn 2014).

Shute, Rieber, and Van Eck (2012) believe that good digital games and good learning environments share similar features—active, goal-oriented, deictic, adaptive, and responsive. Hence, digital games have the potential for supporting the kinds of skills that good learning environments support—critical-thinking and problem-solving skills (Hung and Van Eck 2010); communication and collaboration (Prensky 2006); and self-regulation—or lifelong learning (Rieber 1996). In other words, good digital games are good for 21st-century learning, and transmedia storytelling encompasses the features of good digital games.

Critical Thinking and Problem Solving

Gee (2007b) states that digital games "situate meaning in a multimodal space through embodied experiences to solve problems" (40). However, different types of gameplay require different types of critical-thinking and problem-solving skills, and this holds equally true for transmedia play. Hung and Van Eck (2010) developed a classification system to align problem solving to gameplay using Jonassen's (2000) typology of problems. Jonassen's typology correlates 11 different problem types with a continuum of knowledge and cognitive processes. Of the knowledge and cognitive processes associated with different problem types, metacognitive thinking is a particularly important skill because it acts as an important pathway to critical thinking and problem solving (Magno 2010). Metacognitive thinking is also a primary component of self-regulation, which is requisite for information literacy and lifelong learning. Focusing on metacognitive problems, Table 3.1 adapts Hung and Van Eck's classification system of problem solving and gameplay to transmedia play with examples that potentially support the critical-thinking and problem-solving skills associated with each of the problem types listed.

Communication and Collaboration

In well-designed constructivist learning environments, communication and collaboration function as social negotiation tools to promote the generation of new knowledge and to expose learners to a diversity of viewpoints (Driscoll 2005). Prensky (2006) suggested that digital games can serve as intermediaries for the development of communication and collaboration skills, and relatedly, group decision-making and negotiation skills. Transmedia storytelling further extends

Table 3.1: Metacognitive Problem Types and Supporting Examples of Transmedia Play

Problem Type	Learning Activity	Transmedia Examples
Diagnosis-Solution	Considering multiple possibilities with one best interpretation or solution	<u>Frankenstein MD</u>; <u>Ruby Skye P. I.</u>
Strategic Performance	Using tactical strategies for real-time performance	Star Wars franchise, e.g., Disney parks' *Star Tours—The Adventure Continues*
Case Analysis	Identifying a solution and arguing a position	*Gone Home*
Design	Acting on goals to produce a product	*Ever, Jane*; *Inanimate Alice* (maker activities)
Dilemma	Reconciling multiple perspectives with many possible solutions	*Collapsus*

Note: Alignment based on works by Hung and Van Eck (2010) and Jonassen (2000).

the opportunity for developing such skills through its inherently participatory nature. For example, when individuals produce and share fan fiction, role-play in a virtual world (e.g., *Pottermore*), or form a wiki community around a story (e.g., Star Wars), they are not only contributing to the transmedia storytelling universe but also participating in a community of practice—requiring communication, collaboration, group decision-making, and negotiation skills (Lave and Wenger 2003).

Lifelong Learning

Lifelong learning is characterized by self-direction, also known as self-regulation. Three primary characteristics are present in self-regulated learners: (1) metacognitive awareness, (2) use of appropriate strategies, and (3) motivational control (Zimmerman 2002). Metacognitive awareness permits learners to self-reflect on their own learning, set goals accordingly, and identify the

> " The state of flow is associated with self-regulation, a necessary skill for lifelong learning. As an educational tool, transmedia storytelling has the potential to engage learners in a state of flow. "

best strategies to reach their goals. Motivational control allows learners to maintain the effort needed to reach their goals. In short, self-regulated learning is effective learning.

Rieber (1996) used Piagetian Learning Theory and Flow Theory as frameworks to illustrate the conditions of self-regulated learning in games, situating it within the concept of the microworld. Microworlds can be thought of as small environments where learners build knowledge through play. Digital games are examples of microworlds, as are the multiple story worlds of transmedia universes. According to Piagetian Learning Theory (Ormrod 2012), learning occurs within a state of conflict. Self-regulation is necessary to resolve the conflict. Because the goal of almost any game is to resolve some sort of conflict, the gameplay in transmedia storytelling makes it a natural contender for supporting self-regulated learning. Through gameplay—and more broadly, transmedia play—learners are able to experience conflict on a small scale and work toward an understanding of it. That process of resolving conflict mimics the process of self-regulation.

Flow Theory (Csikszentmihalyi 1990) describes the state that people enter into when they become so absorbed in an activity that time passes without notice and all other distractions disappear. Flow, like self-regulation, requires a high level of motivational control to maintain attention and concentration. The concept of flow has been used to describe both the experience of gameplay (Rieber 1996) and the experience of interactive storytelling (Roth, Vorderer, and Klimmt 2009), signifying that transmedia storytelling is a highly engaging tool. From that standpoint, it can be argued that transmedia storytelling provides the necessary ingredients for increased student engagement and self-regulated learning.

Transmedia Storytelling as Gameplay

Gameplay is a common feature of many transmedia storytelling projects, which reflects a long-held, though contentious, relationship between games and narrative. In the world of game design, there is debate about whether or not games do in fact tell stories. On one side of the debate are the ludologists, who contend that gameplay is about mechanics, not storytelling. On the other side of the debate are the narratologists, who contend that narrative is an inherent part of all games. One well-known narratologist, Janet Murray (2004), argues that "games are always stories, even abstract games such as checkers or *Tetris*, which are about winning and losing, casting the player as the opponent-battling or environment-battling hero" (2). She coined the term *cyberdrama* to describe the type of storytelling that games provide, where participants' actions transform the narrative world to create a sense of immersion in the game. Similar to Murray's concept of cyberdrama is Jenkins's

(2006) concept of transmedia storytelling—an immersive experience that has been brought about by a transformative process in the way media functions (i.e., convergence culture).

Even though the concepts of cyberdrama and transmedia storytelling are similar, when Jenkins weighed in on the debate between ludologists and narratologists, he took a middle ground by concurring that not all games include narrative. He even disagreed with Murray's suggestion that games such as *Tetris* are stories. However, Jenkins did argue that while many games are narrative-based, the experience of gameplay cannot be reduced to mere storytelling. His solution for the debate was to describe the storytelling in games as narrative architecture (Jenkins 2004). The concept of narrative architecture starts with the idea that games are *spatial stories*, which Jenkins likens to the storytelling traditions of odysseys, quests, or travel narratives, where the story worlds are perceived by some as taking precedence over character and plot development. Classic authors such as Jules Verne, J.R.R. Tolkien, and Jack London fall into this category.

When games are designed as spatial stories, they often build upon preexisting narratives that enable players to enter the game with a solid mental map of the characters and situations of a familiar fictional world. For example, the massively multiplayer role-playing game, *Ever, Jane* (everjane.com) is based on the fictional world of Jane Austen. Players who are even remotely familiar with Jane Austen enter the game fully aware that they are more likely to encounter gossip, grand balls, and dinner parties rather than dungeons and dragons during gameplay. *Ever, Jane* is a good example of a spatial story in that the game was built to depict the fictional world of Jane Austen's characters, allowing game players to construct new stories by reenacting their conceptions of the original narrative. In other words, storytelling elements become embedded narratives in the game space and the narrative is enacted through the game players' actions and interactions (Jenkins 2007).

Jenkins's proposal that games are narrative architecture—story worlds built on (often) preexisting narratives that are familiar to players, allowing them to contribute to the narrative by reenacting the story or constructing new stories in the narrative space—is a reflection of the principles underlying transmedia storytelling (i.e., world building, multiplicity, immersion, performance). Taking a middle ground in the debate between ludologists and narratologists allowed Jenkins to create a bridge between storytelling and gameplay. By doing that, he established a narrative connection between games and stories, the foundation on which most transmedia storytelling projects are built. In that light, transmedia storytelling can be thought of as a convergence of the media platforms that deliver gameplay and storytelling. This characteristic makes transmedia storytelling a particularly powerful tool for supporting literacy and learning because both storytelling and games make good tools for learning.

Transmedia Storytelling as a Learning Tool

Transmedia storytelling offers the learning benefits of both storytelling and gameplay, making it a promising tool for a wide range of skills development in formal education. The process of navigating a transmedia story supports core 21st-century skills—critical thinking and problem solving, communication and collaboration, information and related literacies, and lifelong learning. Because of this, transmedia play can be aligned to 21st-century learning standards, including the *Standards for the 21st-Century Learner* (American Association of School Librarians 2007), the *ISTE Standards for Students* (International Society for Technology in Education 2007), and the *Common Core State Standards* (National Governors Association Center for Best Practices and Council of Chief State School Officers 2010). Furthermore, the participatory culture that is characteristic of transmedia storytelling supports the fourth "C" of 21st-century learning—creativity. In short, transmedia play is a 21st-century learning tool.

Transmedia Play as 21st-Century Learning

Transmedia play converges the learning benefits of storytelling with the learning benefits of gameplay, resulting in an educational tool that can act as a bridge that connects the analog with the digital to facilitate 21st-century learning. Multimodal play translates to multimodal reading, thinking, communicating, collaborating, and creating. These same skills are embedded across the range of 21st-century learning standards—a central focus for college and career readiness in most schools today. The value of transmedia play, then, is in its ability to connect traditional learning with digital learning, creating opportunities to reimagine traditional learning activities into 21st-century learning activities. Table 3.2 provides examples of representative learning activities that can be derived from the affordances of transmedia play, illustrating how they fit into 21st-century curricula by aligning them to the *Standards for the 21st-Century Learner* (American Association of School Librarians 2007), the *ISTE Standards for Students* (International Society for Technology in Education 2007), and the *Common Core State Standards* (National Governors Association Center for Best Practices and Council of Chief State School Officers 2010).

The examples of learning activities in Table 3.2 may take place in either formal or informal learning environments. While character analysis is a common activity in the language arts classroom, it may also be undertaken during a book club meeting in the library—or perhaps during

Table 3.2: Transmedia Play Aligned to 21st-Century Learning Standards

Activity	Standards for the 21st-Century Learner	ISTE Standards for Students	Common Core State Standards
Character analysis	1.1.6, 1.1.7	3a., 4a., 4c.	CCSS.ELA-LITERACY. CCRA.R.1; CCSS.ELA-LITERACY. CCRA.R.3
Digital storytelling	2.1.6, 3.1.4, 4.1.8	1b., 2b., 6b.	CCSS.ELA-LITERACY. CCRA.W.3; CCSS. ELA-LITERACY. CCRA.W.6
Cross-curricular research project	1.1.3, 1.1.4, 2.1.1	1a., 3a., 3b., 4a.	CCSS.ELA-LITERACY. CCRA.W.7; CCSS. ELA-LITERACY. CCRA.W.8
Game design	2.1.3, 2.1.4, 4.1.8	1a., 1b., 1c., 6a.	CCSS.MATH. PRACTICE.MP2; CCSS.MATH. PRACTICE.MP4; CCSS.MATH. PRACTICE.MP5

a transmedia fiction club meeting. In both cases, transmedia play is the tool used for digging deeper (drillability) into the details of the story's characters. By the same token, research projects (transmedia navigation) are common across many school-related subjects, but may be equally suitable in the library as an activity linked to a summer reading program, digital literacy initiative, or even one-book initiative—with the book being represented by a transmedia story, of course. Finally, both game design and digital storytelling are maker activities (performance), so are equally at home in classroom or library makerspaces; and the storytelling and gaming elements of transmedia play provide an ideal source of inspiration for such activities. As Table 3.2 shows, all four examples of learning activities are well aligned to 21st-century learning standards. The standards also align to each other, sharing common ground in the multimodal skills of the new literacies and new media literacies.

Transmedia Play as Effortful Creativity

Creativity plays a crucial role in supporting lifelong learning. Opportunities to "play" with newly learned concepts by applying them in varied ways and in multiple contexts enhance understanding through meaning-making, thus facilitating transfer of knowledge (Starko 2013). From a cognitive perspective, creativity is associated with both divergent and convergent thinking. Divergent thinking is about alternative approaches to problem solving—thinking about new possibilities or new ways of doing things; convergent thinking is knowledge-based and involves identifying the "most effective" solution to the problem. Traditionally, divergent thinking was thought to be the definitive characteristic of creativity (Cropley 2006). However, the role of convergent thinking in creativity is currently recognized as an important element of effortful creativity, linking knowledge with creativity to arrive at creative achievement (Ericsson and Lehman 1999).

Cropley (2006) argued that convergent thinking is requisite for effective divergent thinking, and proposed an expansion of Wallas's four stages of creativity—Preparation, Incubation, Illumination, and Verification—in an effort to integrate both divergent and convergent processes of thinking. For Wallas (1926), the creative process was a problem-solving process that began with Preparation, the stage at which the problem was thoroughly investigated with the "traditional art of logic" (40). The second stage was Incubation where the problem was left to the unconscious or "subconscious thought" (41). The Incubation stage led to the third stage of Illumination—the "aha" moment in the creative process, brought on by a merger of both the conscious and unconscious thoughts of the previous two stages. The final stage in Wallas's four stages of creativity was Verification, the stage at which the creative idea was both validated and fully developed.

Table 3.3 is an adaptation of Cropley's model (and expansion) of Wallas's four stages of creativity, demonstrating how the different phases of effortful creativity are evident within transmedia play. The skills that Jenkins identified for the new media literacies are integrated into Cropley's model under the heading, Transmedia Play, to illustrate how all phases of effortful creativity are present within the transmedia play experience.

Loertscher and Woolls (2014) recommend transmedia storytelling as a tool for encouraging and supporting creativity in formal education, especially within the context of maker activities and makerspaces. As an adjunct to transmedia storytelling, they suggest the uTEC Maker Model (Loertscher, Preddy, and Derry 2013) to aid teachers and librarians in recognizing and rewarding creative behavior in the classroom and in the library. The uTEC Maker Model describes four categories of behaviors that reflect creativity, as shown in Figure 3.1.

u for Using: Engaging and participating in any or all modalities of the transmedia play experience is an example of using.

Table 3.3: Phases of Effortful Creativity within Transmedia Play

Phase	Activity	Transmedia Play	Creative Thinking
Information	Perceiving Learning Remembering	Distributed cognition	Convergent
Preparation	Identifying problem Setting goals Investigation	Multitasking Transmedia navigation	Convergent
Incubation	Making associations Building networks	Play Negotiation	Divergent
Illumination	Making new configurations	Simulation Appropriation Performance	Divergent
Verification	Checking for relevance and effectiveness	Judgment Simulation	Convergent + divergent
Communication	Acting on feedback	Collective intelligence Networking	Convergent + divergent
Validation	Judging relevance and effectiveness	Judgment	Convergent

T for Tinkering: Modding or making personal changes to a game like *Minecraft* and remixing a transmedia story with a tool like Mozilla's *Popcorn Maker* are examples of tinkering.

E for Experimenting: The trial and error of learning how to build a game or animated short in *Scratch* with the intent of contributing to a transmedia universe is an example of experimenting.

C for Creating: Participation in a transmedia universe through successful contribution to the storyline (i.e., inventing or producing a new story) is an example of creating.

The uTEC Maker Model also identifies underlying dispositions (e.g., problem solving, inquiry, collaboration, communication) that are developed as a result of effortful creativity. These same 21st-century skills are central to key learning standards, including the *Standards for the 21st-Century Learner* (American Association of School Librarians 2007), the *ISTE Standards for Students* (International Society for Technology in Education 2007), and the *Common Core State Standards* (National Governors Association Center for

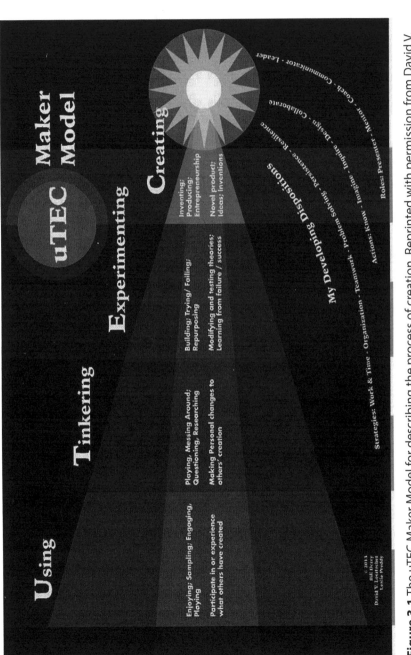

Figure 3.1 The uTEC Maker Model for describing the process of creation. Reprinted with permission from David V. Loertscher.

Best Practices and Council of Chief State School Officers 2010). That makes the uTEC Maker Model an instrument for aiding in the implementation of 21st-century learning behaviors in education; and the transmedia play experience is an excellent vehicle for implementing the uTEC model.

Conclusion

The experience of engagement and immersion that is so characteristic of transmedia storytelling creates a new approach to reading—transmedia play. Multimodal storytelling that harnesses the spatial stories of games with traditional aspects of storytelling packs a one-two punch as a powerful tool that supports both literacy and learning. Moreover, by combining the learning benefits of storytelling with the learning benefits of gameplay to support the four Cs of critical thinking, collaboration, communication, and creativity, transmedia play embodies an ideal tool for 21st-century learning, effortlessly aligning itself to 21st-century learning standards. Perhaps the most overlooked of the four Cs in education today is creativity. Transmedia play offers a remedy for that, and when combined with the uTEC Maker Model, transmedia play can support teachers' and librarians' efforts in bringing creativity front and center into 21st-century classrooms and libraries.

CHAPTER 4

Transmedia Storytelling in the Library

Cataloging and Curating Transmedia Content ▪ A "Third Place" ▪ A "Third Space" ▪ Supporting Multiple Library Goals

While the concept of transmedia storytelling may be a new one for libraries, the underlying elements of transmedia play—namely storytelling and gaming—are not. Storytelling has a long history in libraries as one of the oldest forms of library programming for children (Jenkins 2000). Gaming is not a new concept in libraries either. However, digital games are a more recent trend in libraries—most prominently in public libraries—but increasingly in school and academic libraries as well (Adams 2009). Transmedia storytelling as both gameplay and storytelling fits neatly into this trend, creating new opportunities for libraries to take on the role of supporting 21st-century literacy and learning.

Cataloging and Curating Transmedia Content

Transmedia collections already exist to some extent in libraries. When a library purchases the book(s), the movie(s) or television series, video games, and other materials associated with a story (e.g., Game of Thrones, Star Wars), it is essentially collecting the numerous storytelling platforms of a transmedia franchise. However, curation of transmedia storytelling content requires libraries to recognize the connections between the multiple media platforms in a transmedia franchise and maintain them in a way that links them together and makes them easily discoverable, enabling the library community to find, access, and fully

> **The many manifestations of multiple-narrative transmedia illustrate the increasing necessity of standards like FRBR and RDA for making the discoverability of transmedia storytelling cohesive.**

experience transmedia storytelling universes. Metadata approaches to cataloging have the capability of achieving this.

Making Transmedia Universes Discoverable

The Functional Requirements for Bibliographic Records (FRBR) group of the International Federation of Library Associations and Institutions (IFLA) developed the entity-relationship model of bibliographic records to conceptualize the idea of a standardized bibliographic record that incorporates and identifies all manifestations of a work (Tillett 2004). Figure 4.1 illustrates the FRBR entity-relationship model. These same relationships are equally applicable to transmedia storytelling.

Same expression refers to works that function identically even when platform differs. For example, the hard copy and eBook version of *Harry Potter and the Sorcerer's Stone* represent same expressions. *New expressions* are adaptations of an original work to a new platform. The movie version of *Harry Potter and the Sorcerer's Stone* is an adaptation—very similar in storyline, but expressed through actors rather than text. New expressions do not qualify as transmedia storytelling. On the other hand, *new works* are the embodiment of transmedia storytelling. For example, *Pottermore* is an entirely new manifestation of the Harry Potter story world.

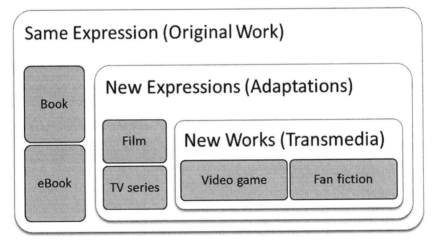

Figure 4.1 The bibliographic relationship of transmedia storytelling.

By making transmedia storytelling discoverable within library spaces, literacy connections between story worlds (e.g., reading and gameplay) can be fostered. A bibliographic record that serves as a single entry point for discoverability of all manifestations of a work is exactly the type of structure needed to catalog transmedia storytelling (Vukadin 2014). When used in conjunction with the unified cataloging standard, Resource Description and Access (RDA), libraries have the opportunity to catalog transmedia storytelling in the way it was intended to be consumed—as a storytelling universe. However, the realization of cataloging works in the context of a bibliographic universe has not yet been made, as many cataloging systems do not currently support RDA. RDA is on the horizon though, as was demonstrated at the first ever *Jane*-athon, a hackathon for metadata about all things Jane Austen, that took place at the American Library Association's Midwinter Meeting in 2015, which was held in Chicago.

Making Transmedia Play Accessible

It is not enough for a library to merely make transmedia storytelling discoverable through cataloging though. To fully support literacy and lifelong learning through transmedia storytelling, it must be made accessible by providing opportunities to engage in transmedia play within the library. Just as libraries carve out spaces for browsing and reading books, spaces for transmedia play should also be created. However, because transmedia storytelling is defined by its multiple media platforms, multiple spaces within the library may be necessary in order for the community to fully participate in transmedia story worlds.

Spaces dedicated to gaming (or that allow gaming as an activity) are a must-have for creating access to transmedia play. These spaces might include access to multiple gaming platforms (including personal computers), access to headphones, and enough room to accommodate group play. Additionally, makerspaces are important in providing access to transmedia play because spaces that support digital creation allow the community to take part in the participatory culture of transmedia storytelling. Lastly, accessibility to transmedia play requires making the many freely available, independent transmedia storytelling projects more visible within the library community. To make lesser-known indie projects visible to library users, projects might be highlighted on a library's web site, reviewed through a library's weblog, shared through a library's social media platforms, displayed interactively in the library itself, or integrated into library programming (transmedia story times, transmedia fiction clubs, etc.). Transmedia play is immersive, multimodal, participatory, and experiential, making the library's support of it more

A "Third Place"

Third places are informal gathering places outside the workplace (or classroom) and home where individuals can go to socialize. Urban sociologist Ray Oldenburg (1999), who introduced the idea of third places, argued that these "great good places" serve important social and cultural functions in communities by bringing diverse groups together in relaxed settings and providing places for people to take part in leisurely and entertaining activities. In doing so, third places "foster democracy . . . and encourage friendship, understanding and tolerance" (Oldenburg 2001, 17).

The role of libraries as places for the democratic exchange of ideas, providers of free and equitable access to information, venues for pursuing personal and aesthetic growth, and centers for lifelong learning embraces the central philosophy of third places. That is, as "great good places," libraries function as social and cultural institutions in communities that bring diverse groups together and provide places for individuals to take part in a variety of activities.

Transmedia storytelling is an ideal tool for enhancing libraries' roles as third places, in large part due its multimodality and participatory nature. Multimodality supports leisurely reading across multiple platforms, giving individuals the opportunity to experience stories in diverse and entertaining ways. The participatory culture of transmedia storytelling gives individuals equal opportunities to make their voices heard by contributing to the transmedia storytelling universe through their own creations.

Oldenburg (1999) described eight essential characteristics of third places. Both libraries and transmedia storytelling embrace these key characteristics, making them excellent partners in the process of establishing a third place "sense." Table 4.1 describes Oldenburg's (1999) eight essential characteristics of third places in the context of both libraries and transmedia storytelling.

A "Third Space"

The concept of third space (as opposed to third place) has roots in both postcolonialism and educational research. Postcolonialist Homi K. Bhabha (1994) used the term *third space* to describe the ambivalence and hybridity that occurs in locations when changes made by colonized groups disrupt the dominating culture. Gutierrez, Rymes, and Larson (1995) proposed the concept of third space in an academic context, as a social space where the "various cultures, discourses, and knowledges are made available to all classroom participants, and thus become resources for mediating learning" (467). Moje et al. (2004) blended the conceptualization of third space by Bhabha and Gutierrez, among

Table 4.1: Third Places in the Context of Libraries and Transmedia Storytelling

Characteristics	Libraries as Third Places	Third Place Tool
Neutral	Libraries are third places because they act as a neutral territory, where individuals are free to come and go as they please, and where everyone within the community feels an equal sense of "ownership" for the place.	Transmedia storytelling is a third place tool because its participatory nature encourages "ownership" of the story through fan contribution (e.g., fan fiction).
Leveling	Libraries are third places because they are inclusive; all are welcome regardless of age, race, gender, beliefs, or socioeconomic status.	Transmedia storytelling is a third place tool because it encourages anyone and everyone to participate in and contribute to the transmedia storytelling universe.
Social	Libraries are third places because they are social centers and meet-up spaces where people gather to talk, hang out, and share their interests.	Transmedia storytelling is a third place tool because it can serve as the impetus that drives the conversation (e.g., transmedia fiction club).
Accessible	Libraries are third places when they are easy to access and accommodating to individual needs.	Transmedia storytelling is a third place tool because its multimodality makes it both accessible (multiple platforms, multiple entry points) and accommodating (serving multiple interests) to participants.
Repeat Visitors	Libraries are third places because they typically attract a core group of regular users who contribute to the atmosphere of the space.	Transmedia storytelling is a third place tool because it attracts a strong fan base.
Unpretentious	Libraries are third places because they are often unpretentious, being designed with functionality in mind first, rather than aesthetics (though some are certainly aesthetically pleasing).	Transmedia storytelling is a third place tool because even the most utilitarian platforms (e.g., Twine) can be harnessed to create and contribute to the transmedia storytelling universe.
Playful	Libraries are third places because they foster an air of possibility and playfulness.	Transmedia storytelling is a third place tool because it is by nature playful.
Relaxing	Libraries are third places because they are often inviting and relaxed spaces with the express purpose of making visitors want to stay for a while.	Transmedia storytelling is a third place tool because it fully immerses participants in the storytelling experience to the point that they may lose track of time (i.e., state of flow).

others, to create a third space construct, described as the "integration of knowledges and Discourses drawn from different spaces . . . that *merges* the 'first space' of people's home, community, and peer networks with the 'second space' of the Discourses they encounter in more formalized institutions such as work, school, or church" (41). Moje et al.'s construct of third space is not unlike Oldenburg's definition of third place—both share the idea of a social space that is separate from home and work, though one is concrete and one is abstract.

Recognition of the need to merge informal multimodal literacy practices into school-based literacy practices is well established (Jewitt 2008; NCTE 2008; Mills 2011), and the concept of third spaces has been used to explore ways of doing this. For example, a connection between the literacy practices of gaming—so intrinsic to transmedia play—and school-based literacy practices has been made by a number of scholars (Apperley and Walsh 2012; O'Brien and Scharber 2008; Alper and Herr-Stephenson 2013). Harnessing these connections may better engage learners and close the gap that exists between advantaged and less-advantaged children (O'Brien and Scharber 2008).

The multimodality of transmedia play can achieve this goal by providing learners with ways of reading and telling stories that are, at the same time, both familiar and new. Like books, transmedia storytelling is based on systems that must be understood for meaning-making, though in transmedia play meaning-making is multimodal—the player must interpret multiple forms of media. Unlike books, transmedia play can bring "literacy into action" by bridging text with gameplay through paratexts (Apperley and Walsh 2012). Even more so, the actions required for reading across multiple modes of texts—both print and online—are not only demanding of the skills of online reading comprehension but also those of traditional reading comprehension, thus enabling connections between informal and formal literacy practices. In that way, transmedia play serves as a third space that connects traditional print literacy with the new literacies, creating opportunities to foster a critical understanding about the structure and purpose of multimodal texts through an approach that is both engaging and entertaining. Beyond transmedia play, the participatory culture of transmedia storytelling is, by itself, a third space, allowing readers or players to contribute to communities that share fan-produced paratexts (e.g., fan fiction, walkthroughs, mods).

Elmborg (2011) considers libraries to be third spaces, defined as technology-enabled learning spaces that also support the social interactions of learners. An example of this is the learning commons, which is becoming increasingly visible on school campuses (Fisher 2010; Loertscher and Koechlin 2014). Elmborg (2011) suggests that school libraries can serve as third spaces to bridge learners' informal (outside school) and formal (academic) literacy practices. Transmedia play, as a third space, can act as a conduit for making those connections happen within school library spaces. School librarians can blend learners' informal and formal literacy practices by providing access to transmedia resources, sponsoring transmedia fiction or gaming clubs, integrating transmedia storytelling into makerspaces and maker activities, and exploring the uses of transmedia for library instruction. In doing so, transmedia play becomes a third space activity in the library as third space—or more accurately the learning commons as third space.

Supporting Multiple Library Goals

Transmedia storytelling can play an important role in serving the three primary purposes of libraries: social, democratizing, and educational. The participatory culture of transmedia storytelling can support both the social and democratizing roles of libraries, and the multimodal nature of transmedia texts has the potential to support the educational role of libraries.

Social Goals

Libraries have historically served as social centers, both in the community and in the school. Today, libraries host story times, educational programs, gaming events, fiction clubs, maker events, and more to bring like-minded individuals together for socialization. When merging transmedia storytelling with such events, libraries can support a participatory culture of socialization that connects the traditional with the technological in a manner that perhaps better serves the digital generation.

For example, in a transmedia story time, the storyline would unfold across multiple media platforms (e.g., book, props, animation) to create an immersive, multimodal storytelling experience that encourages young children to interact and play with the story, and contribute to the plot. A transmedia fiction club would explore entire storytelling universes, rather than limiting itself to a single storytelling mode (e.g., book). The exploration of multiple media platforms would likely attract a more diverse group of people, giving individuals freedom to choose one or more entry points or ways of participating in discussions about the story. Transmedia gaming events might serve as social campaigns for libraries, taking place across multiple platforms (i.e., physical space, social media, and web site) and bringing individuals together to collectively unravel the clues in the game.

> ❝ Transmedia storytelling is a third place tool, thus serving as an impetus for the social goals of libraries. ❞

> **The participatory culture of transmedia storytelling is, by nature, a democratizing goal.**

Democratizing Goals

Democratization means equity of access, and is a traditional value of libraries. The American Library Association (2015) defines equity of access as the ability for all people to "obtain information in a variety of formats" and to "exercise their right to know without fear of censorship or reprisal" (n.p.). Gee (2012) sees libraries as equitable providers of access in the digital age. Just as libraries have served that role for reading, Gee suggests, they can also serve as the social equalizers for the multiple literacy skills of the 21st century. By providing access to transmedia storytelling sources and opportunities to participate in transmedia play activities (e.g., transmedia story times, transmedia fiction clubs, and maker activities), libraries can support Gee's vision of digital equity.

Democratization is also associated with civic engagement. A Pew Internet and American Life Project report titled *Teens, Video Games and Civics* found that civic gaming experiences among teens correlated strongly with youth's civic engagement in the community (Lenhart et al. 2008). Civic engagement in gameplay was defined as opportunities where players helped or guided other players, participated in guilds, learned about social issues, or struggled with ethical issues. Organizations like Games for Change (gamesforchange.org) foster this type of civic engagement by supporting and curating games that are socially impactful. Two transmedia games curated by Games for Change—*Collapsus* and *Gone Home*—are examples of how transmedia storytelling is becoming an increasingly popular platform for civic-minded games. Civic literacy is a 21st-century literacy, so when libraries support civic engagement through transmedia play, they not only serve their primary mission of democratization but they also support 21st-century learning.

Activism is a part of participatory democratization, and the fan activism of transmedia storytelling opens up new avenues for civic engagement. Brough and Shresthova (2012) define fan activism as "fan-driven efforts to address civic or political issues through engagement with and strategic deployment of popular culture content" (para. 2.3). A successful example of fan activism is the Harry Potter Alliance (HPA; thephalliance.org), an organization of more than 100,000 members across the globe. The HPA works with mainstream activist and charity organizations to raise awareness and funds for local and global causes. For example, the group raised $123,000 for Partners in Health to send medical supplies to Haiti after the earthquake. Through its annual Accio Books campaign, HPA has collected over 200,000 books for communities around the world (Jenkins

2012). The connections to favorite characters and fictional worlds make libraries natural agents for supporting civic engagement through the fan activism of transmedia storytelling.

Educational Goals

Libraries have traditionally provided access to books and other sources to promote educational goals. Providing access to transmedia storytelling can do the same by supporting 21st-century literacy and learning. The experience of reading a transmedia story—transmedia play—not only promotes reading in and of itself but also inspires readers to check out library books with similar themes and genres. Transmedia franchises are the most obvious example of this phenomenon (e.g., Game of Thrones). Similarly, as has been found with digital games, other types of transmedia play (e.g., interactive fiction, transmedia games, transmedia web series) may also serve as a "hook" to help readers find books that match their transmedia storytelling interests. For example, The Lizzie Bennet Diaries might be used to introduce readers to Jane Austen's *Pride and Prejudice*. *Collapsus* might be used to spark a reader's interest in climate fiction—or "cli-fi" for short. Readers who love *Inanimate Alice* might also enjoy *Tokyo Heist* by Diana Renn.

By increasing a learner's interest in a topic, transmedia storytelling can serve as a tool that motivates inquiry, information seeking, and research skills development. For example, Ruby Skye P.I. might be used to increase learners' interest and engagement in topics related to media literacy and digital citizenship (e.g., recognizing spam). *Rockford's Rock Opera* might be used to stimulate learners' curiosity about the topics of ecology and extinction. Frankenstein MD might be used to spark learners' (especially girls') interests in careers in science and medicine. In short, transmedia storytelling has the potential to play an important role in libraries as a tool that inspires a curiosity for learning.

Conclusion

Transmedia storytelling as the convergence of the age-old tradition of storytelling with the technology-rich affordances of new media platforms creates

> **The multimodality of transmedia storytelling can support the literacy goals of libraries; and by providing an immersive experience that fosters deep curiosity, transmedia storytelling can support the lifelong learning goals of libraries.**

an innovative form of fiction that has as much a place in libraries as books and movies and music. To some extent, libraries are already collectors of transmedia storytelling when they purchase the books, the movies, and the video games that express a storytelling universe. However, only through cataloging and curation techniques that improve discoverability (e.g., FRBR, RDA), and through spaces (e.g., game spaces, makerspaces) that improve accessibility, will libraries realize the full impact of transmedia play on the library as a third place—and a third space. Transmedia play can also support the social, democratizing, and educational goals of libraries through a participatory culture that brings individuals together to communicate, collaborate, create, and collectively solve problems. In short, transmedia storytelling has the capacity to truly support the library's greater roles and goals within society.

PART 2

Library Programming and Technology Planning

CHAPTER 5

Transmedia Programming Ideas

To fully embrace the concept of transmedia storytelling as a tool that supports the social, democratizing, and educational goals of libraries, and as a tool that can build bridges between informal and formal literacy practices (i.e., third space), programming that fosters transmedia play should be an essential part of every library's programming repertoire. Building on the theories and concepts introduced in the first part of this book, and employing different examples of transmedia storytelling that were described in previous chapters, Chapter Five provides step-by-step guidance on planning, preparing, and implementing a wide variety of transmedia-inspired library programs that appeal to both children and young adults, and that can be adapted to both public and school libraries.

Many of the program examples in this chapter are rooted in traditional library programming, but with a 21st-century twist. Additionally, when suitable, alignments to 21st-century learning standards are identified, including the *Standards for the 21st-Century Learner* (American Association of School Librarians 2007), the *ISTE Standards for Students* (International Society for Technology in Education 2007), and the *Common Core State Standards* (National Governors Association Center for Best Practices and Council of Chief State School Officers 2010).

To assist in navigating this chapter, a table of contents of program examples is provided as follows:

Transmedia Story Time

If transmedia storytelling is the telling of a story across multiple media channels, then in a transmedia story time, children experience the traditional "read-aloud" through more than one media platform. In addition to book and voice, librarians might use props, sound effects, digital elements, and music to relay the story. Each element becomes a part of the story, and all the elements together tell the whole story. Children come to understand the story by experiencing the collective elements.

Arguably, the typical library story time today already uses multiple media elements. Puppets, songs, pictures, and even costumes represent different media elements, so in essence, a library story time may very well be multimedia in nature. However, the difference between multimedia and transmedia is in the way the various media elements work together. Multimedia means multiple media elements. Transmedia means across media elements. Multimedia is often used to engage and entertain children during story time. Transmedia can achieve the same effect, with the understanding that each media element is selected and used intentionally to tell a part of the story. Transmedia story times have the potential to truly embody the concept of transmedia play, but in order to do so, at least three of the characteristics of transmedia play as discussed in Chapter Three must be present in order to transform library story times into transmedia story times: (1) three or more modalities that uniquely contribute to the narrative, such as images, animation, and song (i.e., accessibility); (2) at least one modality that is digital (i.e., mobility); and (3) interactivity that promotes audience participation in the story, such as acting or role-play (i.e., sociality).

From a literacy perspective, transmedia story times have the power to promote and develop comprehension in a way that multimedia alone cannot accomplish, because with transmedia the use of specific media elements is both deliberate and cohesive. That characteristic has the potential to better develop early comprehension skills than the use of multimedia alone. Another reason to implement transmedia story times in the library is that children are already consuming transmedia in their daily lives. Take *Sesame Street* as an example. *Sesame Street* is no longer just a children's television program. Children can now experience the world of Sesame Street through other avenues, including books, eBooks, toys, videos, and story and game apps. Sesame Street has become a transmedia entertainment franchise and is a good representation of how children are informally practicing literacy in their daily lives. Thus, bringing transmedia experiences into a library's story time program creates connections between those informal literacy practices and the more formal literacy practices that story times currently promote, creating a third space effect (see Chapter Four).

The ubiquity of the transmedia entertainment franchises for children—think PBS—makes for a wide field of choices in developing transmedia story time programs. However, single-narrative transmedia, such as interactive fiction, can be simpler to adapt to story time programs because those types of projects exist as complete transmedia storytelling units. In other words, with something like interactive fiction, you only need one project or platform to create a transmedia story time. On the other hand, because multiple-narrative transmedia is dispersed across separate platforms, more than one platform is needed to create a transmedia experience. Because of those differences, this section provides two program examples to serve as templates for transmedia story time program planning: (1) a story time using the interactive fiction project, *Rockford's Rock Opera*; and (2) a transmedia franchise story time that uses multiple storytelling platforms based on Dr. Seuss's *Cat in the Hat*.

Program Example 1: *Rockford's Rock Opera*

Synopsis. This story tells the tale of Rockford the Dog and his human, Moog, and their adventures on the Island of Infinity. Rockford first arrives on Infinity floating on a leaf boat from Battersea Park. Stuck to his backside is a Cocklebur Ick, a small sticky creature. When he arrives on the island, Rockford discovers that it is where the last one of every species goes when it becomes extinct. The Cocklebur Ick has arrived because it has become extinct, but Rockford's arrival on Infinity leads him to be mistakenly registered as extinct. This causes the disappearance of all the dogs in the world. When Moog the Human arrives on the island, both he and Rockford must work together to save the world from dogs becoming officially extinct. They do this by stopping Rockford's paw print from being sent to the registrar to be recorded as a fossil.

Program Overview. *Rockford's Rock Opera* is a long story consisting of three or four parts (depending on format) and 16 chapters. The story time program described in this example uses chapter one of part one as a prompt for participatory storytelling followed by dramatic play. In essence, the transmedia storytelling project, *Rockford's Rock Opera*, is used as the framework for the implementation of Paley's storytelling curriculum (as discussed in Chapter Three).

It is highly recommended that this program be developed as a series to fully explore the story, though the example provided is capable of being a stand-alone program that introduces Rockford's story world. Additionally, while the story and themes in *Rockford's Rock Opera* make it an engaging experience for all ages, the activities in this particular program are specifically designed for early literacy development in preschool and lower elementary-aged children.

This story time requires more than simply playing chapter one of *Rockford's Rock Opera* to an audience of children. Step-by-step instructions are included for the transmedia storytelling presentation, a follow-up participatory storytelling activity based on the story world presented, and a dramatic play of the new story—all of which create an experience that allows children to more fully contribute to the storytelling process. Program leaders will enhance the telling of the story through singing and playacting or miming the actions of the characters. This is followed by a participatory storytelling activity that gives children the opportunity to collectively and collaboratively imagine Rockford's next adventure. The final activity in the program is one of dramatic play, giving children the opportunity to act out their newly told story. The activities in this transmedia story time are not only part of an evidenced-based storytelling curriculum (Paley 1990), but they also align beautifully with Jenkins's transmedia storytelling principles of multiplicity, immersion, world building, and performance.

Target Audience: PK-3

Materials and Equipment Needed:

- *Rockford's Rock Opera*, chapter one (available for free on personal computer [PC], Mac, and iPad; rockfordsrockopera.com)
- Projector screen, computer projector, PC or Mac, speakers
- Internet access for streaming or DVD-ROM
- Two microphones (suggested for larger audiences)
- Alternatively, an iPad with wireless projector if equipment is available
- Whiteboard and markers
- Imaginative dress-up props for story characters such as dog ears and tails, star stickers, scarves, and so on; additional props such as balls, foam noodles, construction paper, or other items that can be used for dramatic play
- Two adults to lead the program

Step-by-Step Instructions:

Planning and Preparation

1. The two program leaders need to become very familiar with the characters of Rockford and Moog in the story, as well as learn the lyrics to the song in Chapter One.
2. Equipment should be set up ahead of time and tested. The projector, PC, speakers, and screen will be used to stream or play Chapter One of the story.
3. Microphones for the program leaders are recommended, especially for larger audiences—the program leaders will be singing along and miming during initial presentation of the story.
4. Dress-up and dramatic play props should be gathered and placed in large open bin(s) for easy access by the audience.

5. It is also recommended that the two program leaders run through the program prior to the event to ensure a smooth performance within the allotted time frame.

Implementation

1. Start the program by introducing the backdrop to the story as a way to gain the children's attention. Example dialogue: "Hello! We have a very special story to share with you today. It is about a dog named Rockford who goes on an amazing and magical adventure. This story is special because you get to help tell it! But first, we need to introduce you to Rockford and his boy named Moog. Let's get started!" (2–3 minutes)
2. The end of the dialogue is a cue to begin playing the story. (12 minutes)
3. Sing along with the songs. Part of the story includes text on screen. Draw the children's attention to the words on screen. You can also dance along.
4. Program leaders can begin miming the action of the story after the sing-along text segment. This enhances comprehension. For example:
   a. Moog kicking around a soccer ball.
   b. Rockford finding the Cocklebur Ick stuck to his backside (children will love this).
   c. Rockford drifting away on the leaf boat.
   d. Moog calling for Rockford as he drifts away.
5. Draw the children's attention back to the screen for the Tale of the Cocklebur Ick.
6. When Chapter One is over, one program leader should ask the audience: "what do you think happens next?" Using the whiteboard, the other program leader should begin writing down the story that the children tell. Storytelling will be collective and collaborative (and very imaginative)— think of it as an exercise in storyboarding. To keep the children on task with the exercise, they may need to be prompted with guiding questions. After 10–15 minutes, wrap up the exercise. Ideally, the new story should have a beginning, a middle, and an end.
7. Begin reading the new story (some of this may need to be ad-libbed). As the story is read, allow the children free play to dramatically act out the story with the props. (15 minutes)
8. At the end of the program, program leaders may wish to hand out Icky Stickers (stickers of the Cocklebur Ick) to children as they leave. Sticker templates are available on the web site (rockfordsrockopera.com).

<u>Note to School Librarians:</u> This type of activity can be adapted to the school curriculum to meet standards for reading, writing, and presentation skills. For example, older students could develop a multimodal musical based on *Rockford's Rock Opera* and present it to younger students as a form of transmedia story time.

Learning Standards Alignments Include:

Common Core State Standards	Standards for the 21st-Century Learner	ISTE Standards for Students
CCSS.RL.5.7	4.1.3	3.a, 3.b, 4.a, 4.c, 5.b
CCSS.W.5.3	3.1.3	2.a, 2.b, 2.c, 4.b
CCSS.SL.5.5	1.2.3, 2.16, 3.13, 3.14	1.a, 1.b, 2.b, 6.b

Program Example 2: Dr. Seuss's *Cat in the Hat*

Synopsis. Sally and her brother are home alone on a cold, wet day. Their boredom ends when the Cat in the Hat appears and wreaks havoc.

Program Overview. Dr. Seuss has become a transmedia franchise. As a result, children can experience different stories about Dr. Seuss's characters through multiple media outlets, including books and eBooks, television, video, merchandise, online games, and printable activities through both the Seussville and PBS KIDS web sites. The sheer amount of media that accompanies transmedia franchises such as Dr. Seuss can be overwhelming when it comes to planning a transmedia story time. The process is made more manageable by focusing on the three basic elements of a transmedia story time. For this program example, the three basic elements are (1) multiple modalities of the story, including the print book or eBook, video clip of the theme song introduction to the *Cat in the Hat Knows a Lot about That* PBS program, and a Cat in the Hat costume and props; (2) digital modalities that include the video clip and eBook; and (3) interactivity that comes from the Cat in the Hat character coming to life, acting out the story, and interacting with the audience.

Target Audience: PK-K

Materials and Equipment Needed:

- *Cat in the Hat* print book or eBook (eBook displayed on the projector screen is preferred so that children can see the words as the story is being read)
- Clip from the *Cat in the Hat Knows a Lot about That* PBS program (available on pbskids.org/catinthehat)
- Projector screen, computer projector, PC or Mac, speakers
- Internet access

- Microphones are recommended
- Alternatively, an iPad with wireless projector if equipment is available
- Dress-up props for Cat in the Hat character
- Additional props that represent items from the story, for example, books, fish, balls, dishes
- Name tags for each child, labeled Thing 1, Thing 2, Thing 3, Thing 4, and so on
- Two adults to lead the program

Step-by-Step Instructions:

Planning and Preparation

1. One program leader will need to dress up as the Cat in the Hat. The other program leader will act as the narrator.
2. The projector, PC, speakers, and screen will be used to stream the beginning theme song clip from the *Cat in the Hat Knows a Lot about That* PBS program.
3. Equipment will also be used to display the eBook (preferably) while the story is being read.
4. A microphone for the narrator is recommended, especially for larger audiences.
5. A Cat in the Hat costume for one of the program leaders should be prepared. It can be as simple as a hat, red scarf, white mittens, and whiskers.
6. Props for acting out the story should be selected, gathered, and placed in bin(s).
7. Equipment should be set up and tested.
8. It is recommended that the two program leaders run through the program prior to the event to ensure a smooth performance within the allotted time frame.

Implementation

1. Provide each child with a "Thing" nametag (i.e., Thing 1, Thing 2. Thing 3, etc.) as he or she enters the story room.
2. Start the program with the narrator reading the introductory section to the book, up until "something went bump!" The program leader playing the Cat in the Hat should be outside the room. (2 minutes)
3. Next, the narrator should begin playing the theme song clip from the *Cat in the Hat Knows a Lot about That* PBS program. (30 seconds)
4. As the theme song ends, the Cat in the Hat character should enter the room.
5. In the meantime, the narrator should begin projecting the eBook pages of the story on the overhead screen, and resume narration.
6. As the narrator reads the story, the Cat in the Hat character should act out the scenes with selected props. (5 minutes)

7. When Thing 1 and Thing 2 are introduced into the storyline, the Cat in the Hat character should bring the audience members with nametags labeled as Thing 1 and Thing 2 to the front of the room. (2 minutes)

8. The narrator should then stop the story and begin the following dialogue (you are also free to develop your own dialogue): "It's not just Thing 1 and Thing 2. No it's not! [Number of children in audience] "Things" are taking over the plot!" At this point, each child in the room will become a "Thing" character in this slight departure to the story.

9. The program leader playing the Cat in the Hat character should encourage the children in the audience to behave like the "Things" (i.e., Thing 1 and Thing 2), making a mess with provided props. (10 minutes)

10. Meanwhile, the narrator should resume the story, ad-libbing if necessary. (Note: "Things" might get a bit wild.)

11. At the end of the story, the audience "Things" should be encouraged to help clean up the "mess" and restore order. (10 minutes)

12. At the end of the program, program leaders may wish to hand out Cat in the Hat coloring pages or stickers to the children as they leave. Free templates are available on pbskids.org/catinthehat.

Note to School Librarians. For K-3, school librarians might consider developing a transmedia version of a Dr. Seuss story time to promote early literacy and technology skills. Though, a modified version would most likely be necessary. For example, instead of acting out the role of "Things" as audience members, students could participate in the storytelling experience by becoming storytellers themselves and collectively imagining and creating new adventures for Thing 1 and Thing 2 (e.g., what happens when they go back in the red box?). With their teacher's assistance, students might produce a class-wide digital storytelling project using such elements as pictures, text, animation, and sound.

Learning Standards Alignments Include:

Common Core State Standards	Standards for the 21st-Century Learner	ISTE Standards for Students
CCSS.RL.3.3	1.1.7	1.a, 3.a, 3.b, 4.a, 4.c
CCSS.W.3.3	3.1.3	2.a, 2.b, 4.b, 5.b, 6.a

Transmedia Fiction Club

So many popular stories today have developed into transmedia franchises by way of movie or television, comic books, fan fiction, video games, merchandise, and more. The James Bond series, Harry Potter, the *Lord of the Rings* trilogy, the <u>Hunger Games</u> books, *Game of Thrones*, and the <u>Sookie Stackhouse</u> series are all examples of novels, or series of novels, that have morphed into transmedia storytelling enterprises. Because books are central to so many of these enterprises, the discussion and exploration of popular fiction in the context of transmedia make a natural addition to library book clubs. Single-narrative transmedia takes this concept one step further by creating opportunities to discuss a new genre in literature.

Whereas the traditional book club focuses primarily on book-centered storytelling, the transmedia fiction club allows patrons to critically examine, explore, and participate in the storytelling experience through multiple media outlets. Transmedia fiction clubs can encompass any, or all, of the following iterations: (1) a club that focuses on single-narrative transmedia storytelling projects, (2) a club that focuses on multiple-narrative transmedia storytelling projects, (3) a transmedia gaming club, or (4) a fan fiction club. Like traditional book clubs, transmedia fiction clubs are an excellent way to promote reading and literacy. Yet, transmedia fiction clubs go beyond traditional literacy. Through the exploration of multiple media outlets, transmedia fiction clubs promote multiple literacies—digital, media, visual, critical, and information literacies.

Because of their complexity, the multiple narratives of transmedia entertainment franchises offer a wealth of material for transmedia fiction clubs. For example, with multiple story outlets to explore, each meeting might build upon the previous meeting in terms of discussing the continuity of story and character, as well as differences in plot, setting, and affect. Club members might start out by discussing the book, followed by discussing the movie in relation to the book, the video game in relation to the book and movie, and so on. Single-narrative transmedia projects can also be explored in the transmedia fiction club, with the primary difference being in the structure of discussion. Discussion of single-narrative transmedia projects must be done holistically, looking at all media elements at once. For example, a transmedia storytelling project that is structured like chapters in a book can be treated in the same way as a book for discussion purposes.

Transmedia fiction clubs might also focus on transmedia games. Transmedia games represent a particular genre in the gaming world, typically as massively multiplayer online role-playing games (MMORPGs) or alternate reality games (ARGs). They may exist as part of a transmedia entertainment franchise (e.g., *Pottermore*, *Game of Thrones: The Game*), or they may exist as stand-alone games with transmedia storytelling features (e.g., *Gone Home*). A transmedia gaming club can act as a community of practice for gamers with specific interests in MMORPGs or ARGs. However, with transmedia gaming, the opportunity for discussion extends beyond gaming. Transmedia gaming clubs also offer opportunities for discussion of narrative or storyline, allowing librarians to create connections between gaming and reading.

Fan fiction may also serve as the focus of a transmedia fiction club and act as a community of practice for writers of fan fiction. Fan fiction itself serves as part of the transmedia experience, allowing people to participate in the storytelling process. By sponsoring a fan fiction club as a type of transmedia fiction club, libraries are not only supporting literacy but they are also supporting what might be described as transmedia literacy.

Because of differences in planning considerations, transmedia fiction club program examples are provided for both a smaller scale transmedia storytelling project, The Lizzie Bennet Diaries, and a larger scale transmedia franchise, Game of Thrones. Program examples for transmedia gaming clubs and fan fiction clubs are also included in this section.

Program Example 1: The Lizzie Bennet Diaries

Synopsis. The Lizzie Bennet Diaries is a transmedia web series that retells Jane Austen's *Pride and Prejudice* through the contemporary lens of a diary vlog. Lizzie Bennet is a 24-year-old graduate student who is still living at home with her parents and two sisters due to owing a great amount of student debt. When wealthy medical student, Bing Lee, and his even wealthier friend, William Darcy, move in nearby, Lizzie's mother goes on a match-making mission. The story unfolds over the course of 100 brief YouTube episodes, as well as through the social media platforms, Twitter and Tumblr.

Program Overview. In this transmedia fiction program, The Lizzie Bennet Diaries is used as a platform for introducing readers to Jane Austen's *Pride and Prejudice*. Meeting activities include discussing the vlog episodes, reading excerpts from the book, discussing the similarities and differences between the original work and Pemberley Digital's retelling, and discussing how the social commentary in Jane Austen's novels serves as a springboard for contemporary forms of storytelling.

Target Audience: Young adults and preteens with advanced reading interests

Materials and Equipment Needed:
- A weblog page to promote the club's activities and interests, also allowing for discussion to take place between meetings (optional)
- Discussion questions as follows:

- How did the media elements contribute to your experience of The Lizzie Bennet Diaries? How did that differ from reading the book?
- Which story did you find more engaging—The Lizzie Bennet Diaries or Pride and Prejudice? Why?
- What were the social issues of Jane Austen's time? How were those issues depicted in The Lizzie Bennet Diaries? What similarities and differences did you notice?
- How do you think Jane Austen would react to The Lizzie Bennet Diaries?
- How would you adapt Pride and Prejudice to a contemporary storytelling platform? What type of media platform(s) would you use? Why?

- Index cards
- Computer, overhead projector, speakers, and projector screen
- Internet access
- Copy of Pride and Prejudice for the facilitator
- A program facilitator to run meetings and maintain the optional weblog

Step-by-Step Instructions:

Planning and Preparation

1. Provide participants with copies of Pride and Prejudice (also available as a free eBook online) and link to The Lizzie Bennet Diaries (pemberley-digital.com/the-lizzie-bennet-diaries). Discussion questions should also be provided ahead of time; alternatively, post the information on the club's weblog page.
2. In preparation, the facilitator should have watched The Lizzie Bennet Diaries and read Pride and Prejudice, making notes of possible answers to discussion questions, and creating additional discussion questions.
3. Identify and book the meeting space.
4. Test equipment.

Implementation

1. For those present who did not read the story, give a brief synopsis.
2. Show the first episode of The Lizzie Bennet Diaries on the overhead.
3. Start with discussion questions, going around the room. Refer to the book when necessary.
4. The web may be needed to explore information and answer questions about the background of the story.
5. Hand out index cards and have each person write down a question or comment to be handed in.
6. Discuss questions or comments as remaining time allows.
7. Use the index cards as a tool to continue the discussion through the group's weblog page until the next meeting.

Note to School Librarians. Transmedia storytelling that retells great works of literature, such as The Lizzie Bennet Diaries, plays an important role in school libraries as a tool that can help students make connections to the classics through contemporary means. For that reason, middle school and high school librarians should consider providing access to these types of storytelling platforms as a way to invite students to become fans of the classics. Such works can also be integrated into the language arts classroom and curriculum for lessons on literary analysis.

Learning Standards Alignments Include:

Common Core State Standards	Standards for the 21st-Century Learner	ISTE Standards for Students
CCSS.RL.9–10.7	1.2.3, 4.1.3	1.a, 1.d, 3.a, 3.b, 4.a, 4.c, 5.b
CCSS.RL.9–10.9	4.1.2, 4.1.3	1.a, 3.a, 3.b, 3.c, 4.a, 4.c, 5.b

Program Example 2: Game of Thrones

Synopsis. Game of Thrones is the title of the first of five novels in George R. R. Martin's epic fantasy, Song of Fire and Ice series. The series' complicated plot follows three simultaneous storylines: (1) the Seven Kingdoms, or Westeros, ruled by the House Stark; (2) the Wall, manned by the Night's Watch warriors, and (3) Pentos in the East, ruled by Targaryen. The Game of Thrones franchise has expanded the novels into an HBO series, as well as a virtual role-playing game.

Program Overview. Plenty of libraries have sponsored *Game of Thrones* book clubs, and some libraries have even sponsored Game of Thrones events. A transmedia fiction club differs from those types of library programs in its full exploration of the multiple story worlds that make up the entertainment franchise. In other words, the books, the games, the television series, and other transmedia formats are discussed and explored in relationship to each other in a transmedia fiction club. This takes time. For that reason, it is recommended that transmedia franchises like Game of Thrones be treated as a special interest clubs. This program example provides step-by-step instructions on how the first meeting in a Game of Thrones transmedia fiction club can be structured and implemented.

Target Audience: Young adults and adults

Materials and Equipment Needed:

- A social media group (Twitter is recommended) to promote the club's activities and interests, also allowing for discussion to take place between meetings

- Extra copies of the books and television series (DVD) available for checkout
- A program facilitator to run meetings and manage related social media

Step-by-Step Instructions:

Planning and Preparation

1. Have individuals who are interested in belonging to a Game of Thrones transmedia fiction club sign up for the first meeting.
2. When signing up, individuals should indicate the media avenue(s) in which they have experienced the Game of Thrones franchise (book, television, other).
3. Ideally, the group will include a mix of individuals with various levels of exposure to the franchise, such as (1) those who have read only one or more of the books, (2) those who have only seen the television series, (3) those who have read the books and viewed the television series, and (4) those who are unfamiliar with Game of Thrones, but would like to learn more about it.
4. Identify and book the meeting space.

Implementation

1. If a Twitter group has been established for the club, consider tweeting out highlights from the meeting.
2. Divide participants into the following groups based on their transmedia experiences with Game of Thrones: (1) book only, (2) television only, (3) book and television, and (4) neither book nor television, and so on.
3. Ask each group to work together and come up a with a 140-character synopsis of the story.
4. Have one volunteer from each group post it to the Twitter group.
5. Read each group's synopsis aloud.
6. Comparing each synopsis, what are the similarities and differences? Does the book-only group differ significantly from the television-only group? How do those two groups compare to the group who has experienced both the book series and the television series?
7. Ask the group who has experienced both book and television to describe differences in how the two media avenues engage them in the story.
8. Continue discussion as time allows. Encourage questions from individuals.
9. To prepare for the next meeting, ask that the book-only group begin watching the television series, the television-only group begin reading the book, and so forth. For clubs focusing on transmedia franchises like Game of Thrones, the eventual goal should be that participants critically explore the wide range of narrative through multiple media channels.
10. Continue the discussion on the group's social media page.

Note to School Librarians. Many popular fiction series in today's school libraries have become transmedia entertainment franchises (e.g., <u>39 Clues,</u> <u>Hunger Games, Harry Potter</u>), giving school librarians an opportunity to promote students' multimodal literacy development through programs like transmedia fiction clubs. Multiple storytelling platforms also provide classroom teachers the opportunity for expanding literary analysis lessons. See **Program Example 1: <u>The Lizzie Bennet Diaries</u>** for learning standards alignments.

Program Example 3: *Gone Home*

Synopsis. Katie returns home from a trip overseas to an empty house, a note on the front door, and her family nowhere to be found. This is a single-player game that requires players, in the role of Katie, to investigate the empty house from top to bottom, find clues and piece them together, and ultimately figure out the plot to the story.

Program Overview. The objective of this program example is to demonstrate how a single transmedia gaming club meeting might be structured. *Gone Home* was selected as the game choice because it offers an accessible entry point into transmedia gaming. It can be played in a fairly short period of time, which may feel less intimidating to casual gamers. The overall goal of a transmedia gaming club should be to provide a forum and meeting place for individuals with similar interests to critically explore and discuss a variety of transmedia games, share gaming tips, and generally socialize. In this program example, the game is played in part during the meeting, followed by a casual discussion of the experience.

Target Audience: Young adults and adults

Materials and Equipment Needed:
- *Gone Home* game, available as a download for Windows, Mac, or Linux
- A social media site (a wiki is recommended) to promote the club's activities and interests, also allowing for discussion to take place between meetings
- Computer, speakers, projector, and screen
- Alternatively, computer hooked up to an HDMI TV
- A program facilitator to run meetings and maintain the wiki

Step-by-Step Instructions:
Planning and Preparation
1. Individuals do not need to play the game beforehand, though it is recommended that the library provide access to the game for interested parties.

Others may choose to purchase and play the game on their own devices. However, the program facilitator should become familiar with the game.

2. Sign-up is recommended to plan for group size.
3. For larger groups, projecting the game on an overhead screen is recommended. For smaller groups (<10), the computer hooked up to an HDMI TV will suffice.
4. Become familiar with the game ahead of time. Walkthroughs can be readily found online.
5. Prepare a few question prompts for the discussion portion of the meeting. For example:
   a. How would you describe the gaming experience compared to other games you have played?
   b. Did the transmedia elements (e.g., music) add to or distract from the gaming experience?
   c. What did the game remind you of?
6. Book the meeting space.
7. Test equipment beforehand.

Implementation
1. Have the game ready to go before the meeting begins.
2. At the beginning of the meeting, introduce the game and provide a synopsis. Explain the transmedia characteristics of the game: it combines music and movie-like elements with a central narrative, making it different from other video games.
3. Poll the group to find out who has played the game and who has not.
4. Have a volunteer from the group begin playing game, preferably one who has not played it before.
5. The rest of the group will be spectators, but should help coach the player through the game.
6. Have group members take turns controlling the game.
7. At least three-quarters of the meeting should be devoted to gameplay. The goal of gameplay is to construct the story of the family out of the clues found in various rooms of the house.
8. The last 15–20 minutes should be devoted to discussion about the story.
9. Start with a question prompt: What happened to this family?
10. Encourage the discussion to be group-led.
11. Have the group choose a transmedia game for the next meeting (see resource list in Appendix A).
12. Continue the discussion on the group's wiki. Wikis provide a good format for collecting gaming FAQs for the various games discussed in meetings.

Note to School Librarians: Transmedia games like *Gone Home* support inquiry-based learning (i.e., information seeking, critical thinking, problem solving), so have a place in school libraries' gaming collections. *Gone Home*, in particular, also provides an excellent example of a digital game whose narrative elements give it the capacity to be integrated into the high school language arts curriculum for the purpose of critical, multimodal, and literary analyses.

Learning Standards Alignments Include:

Common Core State Standards	Standards for the 21st-Century Learner	ISTE Standards for Students
CCSS.RL.11–12.1	2.2.2, 2.2.3, 2.4.1	3.a, 3.b, 3.c, 4.a, 4.c, 4.d, 6.c
CCSS.RL.11–12.3, CCSS.RL.11–12.5	4.1.3	3.a, 3.b, 4.a, 4.c, 5.b

Program Example 4: Fan Fiction Club

Program Overview. Fan fiction groups tend to be devoted to a particular story (e.g., Harry Potter, Twilight, Game of Thrones), so libraries may wish to focus more on offering occasional fan fiction writing workshops while also providing a platform for special interest groups to find and meet up with each other. This program example offers ideas for structuring a fan fiction club.

Target Audience: Ages 10–100

Materials and Equipment Needed:
- A library-sponsored weblog devoted to fan fiction writing, with separate forums created for specific fan fiction groups as the need arises.
- Laptops or tablets that can be reserved for groups.
- Meeting space.
- A program facilitator to maintain the weblog and plan occasional workshops.

Program Ideas:
- Plan monthly meet and greets for fan fiction writers to find others with similar interests. Provide a meeting space and food (if allowed). Circulate through the meet-ups to get ideas for resources and programming.
- Contact the local community college or university to find a speaker for a fan fiction writing workshop.

- Host a fan fiction writing contest. Give out awards and prizes in different categories. Highlight the winners' work on the fan fiction weblog.

Interactive Library Display

Displays are a staple of every library, whether showcasing new titles, popular topics, or marking an event such as Banned Books Week. They are an important avenue for connecting library materials and learning opportunities with library users. However, once the material is in the hands of the library user, the connection has been made and the goal of the display has been met. On the other hand, when material meets user in an interactive display, the goal of the interactive display has just begun. As its name implies, the interactive display invites the library user to participate in some way with the materials and sources at hand. With a transmedia storytelling twist, the library user gets to experience the story with an interactive display. In that way, an interactive display feels somewhat like a hands-on exhibit at a museum.

There are two types of interactive displays that can be designed around transmedia storytelling. The first type embraces multiple-narrative transmedia, and the franchises so often characterized by it. Libraries have already dabbled in this type when creating displays that center on a popular story, such as Harry Potter, the Lord of the Rings, or Star Wars. For example, creating a display that includes the books, the movies, graphic novels, video games, and other materials for a storytelling universe like the Lord of the Rings is essentially creating access to the transmedia storytelling experience for that franchise. Though, it still resembles a traditional library display in that it is not interactive. To make the display interactive, a participatory element needs to be added. Space might be created within the display to play one or more of the video games from the Lord of the Rings franchise. Online access to a virtual version of Middle-Earth for library users to explore might also be included in the display. A makerspace might even be part of the display design, allowing library users to create hobbit avatars and share them with the library community.

The other type of interactive display designed around transmedia storytelling utilizes single-narrative transmedia. Unlike multiple-narrative transmedia, which encompasses a multitude of story-based materials to include in the display, single-narrative transmedia stands alone and therefore becomes the central interactive component of the display. Librarians then have to determine what additional materials to include in the display that will enhance the central story. Those decisions should be based on the themes and affordances of the transmedia storytelling project. For example, *Inanimate Alice*, a series of episodes described as a "born-digital novel," follows the adventures of a girl named Alice as she travels the world with her family from China to Russia to Italy to England. An interactive display featuring *Inanimate Alice* would put the story at center stage, creating a space for library users to interact with it digitally. Additionally, the display might include materials about the various countries and cultures in Alice's travels, along with a world map where library users can try to figure out and pinpoint the exact location of Alice's whereabouts in each episode.

Because interactive displays for single-narrative and multiple-narrative transmedia require different planning considerations, program examples for each type are included in this section. It should also be noted that location is an especially important decision in planning an interactive display. Foot traffic, target audience, and technology needs are just a few factors that must be considered when determining the ideal location for an interactive display.

Program Example 1: *Collapsus*

Synopsis. The world's energy sources are drying up in this dystopian-like transmedia game that moves the participant through time, from 2012 to 2025. Blending fiction and documentary elements within an alternate reality game world, *Collapsus* allows players to try their hand at manipulating the world's energy supplies in order to help save the future.

Program Overview. *Collapsus* provides a good example for how transmedia storytelling can serve as a focal point for an engaging interactive display. First of all, the story deals with a nonfiction, contemporary issue—the energy crisis—which means that an abundance of library materials are available on this topic to enrich the learning value of the display. Second, the interactivity of the project is very much game-based, allowing participants to experiment and manipulate the storyline through their actions. Success in that process requires good decision-making, and because good information improves the decision-making process, an opportunity arises to showcase library materials. Finally, the project itself is aesthetically beautiful, making it a worthy contender for an interactive library display.

Target Audience: Young adults and adults

Materials and Equipment Needed:
- Long table
- One to two computers or laptops
- Two chairs for each computer or laptop

- Two sets of headphones for each computer or laptop
- Corkboard or whiteboard for display signage; stand or easel, unless wall mounted
- Internet access
- *Collapsus* set as the browser home page
- Library materials about the energy crisis to facilitate decision making in the game
- Game guidance sheets, laminated or in literature holders

Step-by-Step Instructions:

Planning and Preparation

1. Consider setting up the display to coincide with an event such as National Energy Action Month in October.
2. Identify the best location for the interactive display. Consider the following:
   a. *Collapsus* is most appropriate for high school to adult age library users.
   b. Library materials needed for the display are nonfiction.
   c. Technology used might dictate location.
   d. Display should be as centrally located as possible in order to reach the target audience.
3. Create noticeable signage that attracts curiosity. Press kit images available on the *Collapsus* web site can be used as part of the display. Large lettering should be included to invite people to play. For example, signage might be worded as follows: "Could you save the world from an energy crisis? Come play *Collapsus*."
4. Create guidance sheets that include a synopsis of the story, navigation rules for the game, and invitation to use the library materials to "help save the world." Specifying behavioral expectations for interacting with the game and display is also advisable.
5. Set up table and display board.
6. Set up computers or laptops, allowing room for two chairs per computer so that people can play together.
7. Arrange library materials on table for easy access.
8. Provide guidance sheets for each computer being used.
9. Test out equipment before launching display.
10. Make an announcement about the interactive display through the library's social media, newsletter, or other avenues as desired.

Implementation

1. Because the display is interactive, be prepared to provide assistance as necessary.

2. Library materials may disappear during the course of the display, either to be checked out or to be reshelved. Add more resources to the display as the need arises.

3. Offer occasional demonstrations of *Collapsus* to garner interest and pique curiosity. You may also wish to use the demonstrations as an opportunity to talk about transmedia storytelling as a new genre.

4. If the display proves to be particularly popular, consider extending the programming by bringing in a local expert to talk about the energy crisis as a global issue.

5. Consider setting up the display to coincide with an event such as National Energy Action Month in October.

Note to School Librarian. This program example has a strong learning value, which makes it a good fit for high school or college library displays. Additionally, transmedia projects that blend fiction with fact can be integrated into the classroom and curriculum to meet learning objectives that address point of view and information literacy. For example, *Collapsus* can be used as an agent of inquiry for pro-con projects that target source evaluation skills and evidence-based analysis.

Learning Standards Alignments Include:

Common Core State Standards	Standards for the 21st-Century Learner	ISTE Standards for Students
CCSS.RH.11–12.3	2.1.3	3.a, 3.c, 4.a, 4.c, 4.d
CCSS.RH.11–12.7	1.1.7, 1.2.3, 2.1.6, 3.1.4	1.a, 2.a, 2.b, 3.b, 3.c, 4.d, 5.b, 6.b

Program Example 2: Star Wars

Synopsis. The Star Wars transmedia franchise is considered a benchmark example of multiple-narrative transmedia storytelling. Centered on George Lucas's film series, the franchise is made up of a multitude of storytelling platforms, including novels, comic books, video games, television series, action figures, and even theme park attractions at Disneyland and Disney World.

Program Overview. Star Wars was selected for this program example not only because it is popular but also because the sheer scope of materials that make up the franchise create an endless variety of possibilities for developing interactive displays. Additionally, a good number of libraries already own Star Wars materials in their many formats. That makes this example a good starting point for libraries to begin experimenting with transmedia storytelling programming. When planning for an interactive display that showcases transmedia franchise materials, the goal should be to select stories in which the library already owns multiple platforms.

Target Audience: All ages

Materials and Equipment Needed:

- Table
- One to two tablets that include a stop-motion app, for example, LEGO Movie Maker (iOS), iMotion (iOS), Stop-Motion (Android)
- Props that can be used to create stop-motion Star Wars video shorts, for example, action figures, LEGOs, backdrops
- Image-rich sources that can be used to inspire the Star Wars videos, for example, graphic novels, comic books, reference books
- Method to display library materials, for example, tabletop book easels, mobile book stand
- Library YouTube account
- Display signage that invites library users to create a Star Wars themed stop-motion video
- Guidance sheets for the activity
- Optional: A touch screen television or large monitor central to the display for showcasing participants' completed video creations

Step-by-Step Instructions:

Planning and Preparation

1. Consider setting up the display to coincide with an event such as a *Star Wars* anniversary.
2. Identify the best location for the interactive display. Consider the following:
   a. Star Wars is popular with all ages.
   b. Creating video shorts is a good group activity.
   c. Library materials needed for the display are both fiction and nonfiction.
   d. The display should be located in an area where group activity already takes place.
   e. The display should be located away from quiet areas, as the activity might cause distracting noise.
   f. An optimal location would be a makerspace area, effectively building a bridge between traditional and innovative library functions (i.e., print and digital tools).

3. Create noticeable display signage that attracts curiosity. Keep copyright law in mind when selecting images or clip art for the display signage.

4. Create guidance sheets that include a description of the activity; instructions for accessing tablets (e.g., where to check them out); directions for using the stop-motion video app; and rules and behavioral expectations for interacting with the display. Consider setting time limits as part of the rules.

5. Optional: Set up touch-screen television or large monitor to showcase video shorts.

6. Set up table with a variety of props that can be used to create stop-motion video shorts.

7. Arrange library materials on or near the table for easy access.

8. Test-run the activity before launching the display.

9. Make an announcement about the interactive display through the library's social media, newsletter, or other avenues as desired.

Implementation

1. Because the display is interactive, be prepared to provide assistance as necessary.

2. As video shorts are created and saved on the tablets, export them to the library's YouTube account so that they can be shared with the library community.

3. If at all possible, it is recommended that the optional touch-screen television or large monitor be used in the display as an additional interactive element, as well as an inspirational tool for other activity participants.

4. Encourage cooperation and collaboration among participants to maximize opportunities for participation.

5. Library materials may disappear during the course of the display, either to be checked out or to be reshelved. Add more resources to the display as the need arises.

6. If the display proves to be particularly popular, consider making it permanent, or expanding upon it with other multiple-narrative transmedia stories.

Note to School Librarians: Interactive displays like the one in this program example would work particularly well in school libraries that house makerspaces. They provide an opportunity for making connections between traditional literacy and 21st-century literacies (i.e., third space effect).

Learning Standards Alignments Include:

Common Core State Standards	Standards for the 21st-Century Learner	ISTE Standards for Students
CCSS.RL.3.9	1.1.7	1.a, 3.b, 3.c, 4.a, 4.c, 6.b

Transmedia-Inspired Maker Program

Makerspaces are currently a big trend in libraries, offering a wide assortment of maker activities, running the gamut from science experiments to technology creations to traditional crafts. Transmedia storytelling is a natural fit for makerspaces. Its multiple story worlds can serve as an inspiration for a well-developed maker program, cohesively planned around a central theme or storyline. Transmedia storytelling may in fact be unique in its ability to spin off so many maker activities that, taken together, allow participants to gain a much fuller experience in the story. In other words, transmedia-inspired maker programs foster greater exploration of the story world.

Cohesive development of a transmedia-inspired maker program requires more than the planning of multiple maker activities inspired by the story worlds. Something is needed to tie the individual maker activities together to give participants a feeling of becoming an important asset in the transmedia storytelling experience. Digital badging is one way to accomplish that goal. By creating digital badges that represent various achievements or levels of participation in the transmedia storytelling experience, individuals become active participants in the story. Digital badges serve two purposes when used in conjunction with a transmedia-inspired maker program. They are earned as the result of accomplishing a certain set of tasks or learning new skills from the maker activities. These skills have value in and of themselves (e.g., learning to code to create a game). They are also earned as the result of achieving a certain level of contribution to the story world (e.g., adding new elements to the story world in a digital story).

While the multiple storytelling platforms of transmedia franchises offer a wealth of inspirational ideas for maker programs, transmedia storytelling projects, such as interactive fiction, may serve as a more manageable starting point for spinning off maker activities from the story. That is, with a strong central narrative, it is easier to plan maker activities that all connect back to it, resulting in a more cohesively planned program. On the other hand, transmedia franchises consist of many different story lines, tied together only by main characters and general plot, making it more difficult to plan and develop maker activities that are tied together around a unified story.

A transmedia-inspired maker program should include the following three basic elements: (1) a transmedia storytelling project with a strong central narrative from which all maker activities are derived, (2) three or more maker activities that highlight different themes or media elements from the project, and (3) a method of situating and unifying the maker activities as important participatory experiences in the central story (e.g., digital badges). Together, those three elements should serve as a solid basis for a well-developed, transmedia-inspired maker program.

While transmedia storytelling can certainly inspire single maker activities in a library's makerspace, single maker activities result in a less immersive experience in the story world. However, they do have a place when used as part of an interactive display, as demonstrated in the Star Wars interactive display example. The program example in this section outlines how the transmedia storytelling project, *Inanimate Alice*, can be used as an inspiration for a maker program consisting of four maker activities with digital badges.

Program Example: *Inanimate Alice*

Synopsis. Alice Field is a globe-trotting girl who has traveled the world with her mother and father, following her father's work in the oil and gas industry. Alice is an only child who wants to be a game designer when she grows up. To keep herself company she creates a digital friend named Brad. The story is told across multiple episodes, with Alice growing up as the story progresses. In episode one, Alice is eight years old. By episode five, she is 16 years old. This transmedia storytelling project is self-described as a "born-digital novel," a work of interactive fiction that allows the reader to drive the story forward through click actions and embedded games.

Target Audience: Grades 3–8

Program Overview. This maker program example takes the themes and affordances of *Inanimate Alice* and translates them into four separate maker activities that are tied to digital badges. Each of the four maker activities allows participants to contribute to Alice's story world in a different way and earn a digital badge to reflect their contribution to the transmedia narrative as follows:

- Getting to know Alice's character and creating an animated short about her earns the Friend of Alice badge.
- Contributing to the adventures of Alice through digital story making earns the Storyteller badge.
- Creating a digital game that Alice might like to play earns the Game Maker badge.
- Creating an interactive travel postcard that Alice might send to her friends earns the World Traveler badge.

Before implementing any of the maker activities in this program, take the following steps:

- Create digital badges for each activity with a tool like Open Badge Designer. Sample badges are included for each maker activity on the following pages.
- Create an Inanimate Alice Maker Program web page specifically for showcasing participants' earned digital badges and projects for the various maker activities.
- Create a space where library users can view *Inanimate Alice*. Any computer that has a Flash-enabled and Unity capable browser will work for this purpose. Getting library users interested in Alice prior to the first maker activity will create a fan base for the entire maker program.
- Make headsets available for viewing the sound effects in the story.
- Use posters to advertise the story and draw library users to the Inanimate Alice web site. Free poster-sized images are available on the project's web site.

Maker Activity 1: Animation Project

Digital Badge. Friend of Alice

Description. In this activity, participants will get to know Alice, and then make an animated project with Scratch that represents something that Alice likes to do. This maker activity is a good introduction to Alice's character, and can be used in conjunction with single or multiple episodes. If using a single episode, episode one is recommended.

Materials and Equipment Needed:

- Computers or laptops, enough for each participant (activity sign-up recommended)
- *Inanimate Alice* episode one (inanimatealice.com)
- Free Scratch programming application (scratch.mit.edu), web-based or downloadable for offline use
- Internet access
- Location for maker activity
- Post-it notes
- Enough pencils for participants
- One program facilitator

Step-by-Step Instructions:

Planning and Preparation

1. Download Scratch if you wish to work offline; otherwise you will need Internet access.
2. Create an account in Scratch for the library.
   a. Click on Join Scratch.
   b. Create a new username and password (enter password twice).
   c. E-mail is required to register, but is used only to reset a password.
   d. An account is needed in order to share projects. A library account will allow access to embed code for showcasing participants' projects on the library's web site.
3. Create a Studio for Inanimate Alice.
   a. Log in to the library's Scratch account.
   b. In the top right-hand corner, click on the username drop-down menu.
   c. Select My Stuff.
   d. Click on New Studio.
   e. Add title.
   f. Select the box that allows anyone to add projects.
4. Learn the basics of the application for animation so that technical assistance can be offered during the activity. Help guides are available on the web site.
5. During the activity, participants may want to find and use additional images for their backdrops and sprites. They will need to save them to the computer or a flash drive in order to upload them into the Scratch program. Determine how that will be handled.
6. Become familiar with the *Inanimate Alice* episode(s) that will be used to inspire the activity.
7. If the library does not have a formal makerspace, identify a location where the activity can take place (e.g., computer lab, meeting room with laptops).

Implementation

1. Introduce the activity by explaining that participants will need to use their imaginations to envision what Alice looks like; she is never seen in any of the episodes. Tell participants that they will be "animating Alice" to bring her to life.
2. Explain that by taking on the challenge to "animate Alice," each participant will earn his or her first digital badge and become an acclaimed Friend of Alice.
3. Hand out a pencil and few sheets of Post-it notes to each participant.
4. Ask participants what they learned about Alice's character in episode 1 (or from multiple episodes). What does she like to do? What is she afraid of? What words best describe Alice?
5. Ask them to write their thoughts down on the Post-it notes.

6. They can stick the Post-it notes to their computer screens to keep descriptive words about Alice fresh in their minds as they work on their projects.

7. Introduce Scratch and the task to create animation. Show participants how to set up an account:

   a. See instructions under Planning and Preparation.

   b. Have participants write down their usernames and passwords on the Post-it Notes.

8. Let participants get started and troubleshoot their way through the Scratch application. Participants should help each other solve problems. Step in only when absolutely necessary. As a hint, show participants how they can click on Explore to browse others' shared projects, and click on See Inside to learn how the projects work.

9. At the end of the session, show participants how to save, share, and add their projects to the Inanimate Alice Studio.

10. Remind participants that they must share their completed projects in the Inanimate Alice Studio in order to earn a Friend of Alice Badge. To showcase earned digital badges and projects on the library's web site, the following steps must be taken:

    a. Identify and record the Scratch username for each participant in the activity.

    b. Log in to the library's Scratch account.

    c. Go to the Inanimate Alice Studio.

    d. Grab embed code for each participant's project in the Studio.

    e. Embed projects and digital badges to the library's Inanimate Alice Maker Program.

Maker Activity 2: Digital Story Making

Digital Badge. Storyteller

Description. Digital story making extends the transmedia experience by giving participants control of the story as authors. This maker activity allows participants to imagine and create new adventures for Alice using a story-making tool called Storybird. It is recommended that participants view at least the first three episodes of *Inanimate Alice* beforehand.

Materials and Equipment Needed:

- Storybird, free web application that works on any device
- Enough computers, laptops, or tablets for each student (activity sign-up recommended)
- Internet access

- Location for maker activity
- One program facilitator

Step-by-Step Instructions:

Planning and Preparation

1. Set up a free educator's account on Storybird:
   a. Click on Sign up for Free
   b. Select Educator/Teacher
   c. Create username and password (e-mail required)
2. Create a class account:
   a. Give the class a name.
   b. Add participants' names under Learners.
   c. Click on Add Learners.
   d. Create a username for each participant.
   e. Print out login cards to be handed out at the beginning of the activity.
3. Create a "class assignment" for the activity so that participants can submit their stories to it (under Assignments).
4. Learn the basics of creating a Storybird longform or picture book (under Write).
5. If the library does not have a formal makerspace, identify a location where the activity can take place (e.g., computer lab, meeting room with laptops).

Implementation

1. Introduce the activity by prompting participants to think about the parts of *Inanimate Alice* that were not told. What do you think life was like for Alice in China? What do you think happened to Alice between escaping from Russia and moving back to England? How do you think Alice felt when living in Saudi Arabia?
2. Explain to participants that they will get to tell the "untold stories" of Alice using a digital story-making tool called Storybird. In doing so, they will earn their Storyteller badges.
3. Hand out login cards and have participants log in to their accounts in Storybird. They will be asked to change their passwords before gaining access to the class account.
4. Orientate participants to the basics of Storybird:
   a. Show participants how to find the "class assignment" in their accounts. They will use it to publish their stories to the class channel.
   b. Show participants how to get started writing.
5. Let participants troubleshoot their way through the Storybird application. They should help each other solve problems. Step in only when absolutely necessary.
6. At the end of the session, show participants how to save and publish their stories to the class channel (same as class name).

7. Remind participants that they must publish their stories to the class channel in order to earn a Storyteller Badge. To showcase earned digital badges and projects on the library's web site, the following steps must be taken:
   a. Log in to the library's Storybird account.
   b. Go to the class page.
   c. Grab embed code for each participant's story.
   d. Embed stories and digital badges to the library's Inanimate Alice Maker Program.

Maker Activity 3: Game Making

Digital Badge. Game Maker

Description. In this maker activity, participants are challenged to design a game like one of the games Alice shared in the earlier episodes of the story. These are simple games of the type that can be made in Scratch. It is recommended that participants be very familiar with the games from episodes two and three of *Inanimate Alice* beforehand.

Materials and Equipment Needed:

- Computers or laptops, enough for each participant (activity sign-up recommended)
- Free Scratch programming application, web-based or downloadable for offline use
- Internet access
- Location for maker activity
- Post-it notes
- Enough pencils for participants
- One program facilitator

Step-by-Step Instructions:

Planning and Preparation

1. Set up a Scratch account and Studio. Follow instructions from Maker Activity 1: Animation Project.
2. Learn the basics of game making in Scratch so that technical assistance can be offered during the activity. Help guides are available on the web site.
3. During the activity, participants may want to find and use additional images for their backdrops and sprites. They will need to save them to the computer or a flash drive in order to upload them into the Scratch program. Determine how that will be handled.

4. Become familiar with the games in *Inanimate Alice* that will be used to inspire the activity.
5. If the library does not have a formal makerspace, identify a location where the activity can take place (e.g., computer lab, meeting room with laptops).

Implementation

1. Introduce the activity by challenging participants to make a game "just like Alice" using the Scratch application. To qualify as a game, their projects need to include click actions.
2. Explain that by taking on the game-making challenge, each participant will earn a digital badge and become an official Game Maker.
3. Introduce Scratch. Show participants how to set up an account (if they do not already have one):
   a. See instructions under Planning and Preparation, Maker Activity 1.
   b. Have participants write down their usernames and passwords on the Post-it notes.
4. Let participants get started and troubleshoot their way through the Scratch application. Participants should help each other solve problems. Step in only when absolutely necessary. As a hint, show participants how they can click on the Explore button in Scratch to browse others' shared projects, and click on See Inside when viewing a project to learn how the projects work.
5. At the end of the session, show participants how to save, share, and add their projects to the Inanimate Alice Studio.
6. Remind participants that they must share their completed projects in the Inanimate Alice Studio in order to earn a Game Maker Badge. To showcase earned digital badges and projects on the library's web site, the following steps must be taken:
   a. Identify and record the Scratch username for each participant in the activity.
   b. Log in to the library's Scratch account.
   c. Go to the Inanimate Alice Studio.
   d. Grab embed code for each participant's project in the Studio.
   e. Embed projects and digital badges to the library's Inanimate Alice Maker Program.

Maker Activity 4: Interactive Travel Postcard

Digital Badge. World Traveler

Description. This maker activity draws on the theme of world travel in *Inanimate Alice*. Participants are asked to put themselves in the role of Alice to create a postcard that she might send to her friends from one of the many locations that she has lived or visited. The ThingLink application is used to add interactive elements to the postcards. It is recommended that participants view at least the first four episodes of *Inanimate Alice* beforehand.

Materials and Equipment Needed:

- Enough computers, laptops, or tablets for each participant
- ThingLink (web site or app)
- Internet access
- One program facilitator
- Location for maker activity

Step-by-Step Instructions:

Planning and Preparation

1. Set up a free educator's account on ThingLink.
2. Create a group (under Learners) and register the participants taking part in the activity.
3. Print or save the login sheet of IDs and passwords.
4. Learn the basics of ThingLink so that technical assistance can be offered during the activity. A Help link is located at the bottom of the page on the web site.
5. If the library does not have a formal makerspace, identify a location where the activity can take place (e.g., computer lab, meeting room with laptops).

Implementation

1. Introduce the activity by asking participants to imagine what it would be like to visit one of the countries that Alice lived in or visited. Ask them to imagine what kind of postcard Alice might send to a friend about her travels.
2. Explain to participants that to earn their World Traveler badge, they must make a postcard inspired by Alice's travels, and not just a postcard—an interactive postcard using ThingLink.
3. Have participants log in to ThingLink with provided IDs and passwords.
4. Show participants the basic functions of ThingLink.
5. Using an image search tool such as Google Images, show participants how to find copyright-free images of postcards to use as the basis of their projects. In the tablet application, they need to be saved to the photo gallery first. In the web site application, they can be directly added as image URLs.
6. Have participants get started on their projects. Tell them to work with each other to troubleshoot problems in ThingLink.
7. As participants complete their projects, show them how to save their work and add it to the group channel in the class account (Add to Channel link).

8. Remind participants that they must add their projects to the class channel in order to earn a World Traveler Badge. To showcase earned digital badges and projects on the library's web site, the following steps must be taken:

   a. Log in to the library's account through the ThingLink web site.
   b. Log in to the group (under Account, select group name from drop-down menu).
   c. Grab embed code for each participant's story.
   d. Embed stories and digital badges to the library's Inanimate Alice Maker Program.

Note to School Librarians. The activities in this maker program would work well in a school library with a makerspace. They may also be adapted into classroom curricula to meet literacy (digital story making), math (animation, game making), and technology (all maker activities) standards.

Learning Standards Alignments Include:

Common Core State Standards	Standards for the 21st-Century Learner	ISTE Standards for Students
CCSS.RL.6.3, CCSS.W.6.3	3.1.3	1.a, 1.b, 2.a, 2.b, 3.a, 3.b, 4.a, 4.b, 4.d, 5.b, 6.a, 6.b, 6.c
CCSS.RL.6.7.	1.1.6, 4.1.3	1.a, 3.a, 3.b, 4.a, 4.c, 4.d, 5.b, 6.a
CCSS.W.6.6, CCSS.MATH. PRACTICE.MP1–8(e.g., game making, animation)	1.1.8, 2.1.4, 2.1.6, 3.1.4	1.c, 2.a, 2.b,, 3.b, 4.b, 4.d, 5.b, 6.a, 6.c

Transmedia-Inspired Library Instruction

Library instruction is an important ingredient in 21st-century learning. For school librarians, teaching information and related literacy skills is a primary responsibility. For many public librarians, that responsibility may seem foreign. However, cuts in public school library funding and an increase in the number of homeschooled learners are just two factors that are thrusting more public librarians into the spotlight of library instruction.

While a multitude of educational technology tools exist for enhancing library instruction, transmedia storytelling may stand alone in its unique ability to serve as a teaching and learning tool that touches on the multiple literacies of 21st-century learning. Information literacy in the age of the Internet requires learners to exercise digital, media, and visual literacy skills. Transmedia storytelling can serve as an educational tool that not only supports all those literacies but also supports them within the narrative-rich environment of a story world. In that way, transmedia storytelling enhances, entertains, and inspires literacy and learning.

The transmedia projects that are best suited for integration into library instruction include the following characteristics: (1) a strong central narrative that can serve as the basis of problem-based learning activities, (2) themes that motivate learners to want to learn more, (3) an age-appropriate storyline that learners can connect to, and (4) multiple media platforms tied strongly to the central narrative. All of the single-narrative transmedia projects introduced in this book fit those characteristics, and would serve as excellent tools for library instruction programs. The following examples illustrate how that can be done:

- *Rockford's Rock Opera*: The theme of ecology offers a good entry point for elementary-aged learners to research, explore, and critically discuss issues about extinction and the environment. By exploring the map of the Island of Infinity and all of its inhabitants on the project's web site, learners can exercise their abilities to sort fact from fiction, and then expand their understanding of the factual parts of the story through research activities.

- *Collapsus*: Both the energy crisis theme and the simulated environment of the game create an excellent platform for targeting research, reasoning, and scholarly discussion skills in older high school and college-level learners.

- *Inanimate Alice*: The themes of world travel and the environmental, ethical, and political issues related to the oil industry that are subtly woven throughout the story can be used to foster research and debate skills at the middle school or high school level.

Because transmedia franchises exist across many separate platforms, they do not fit the characteristics listed earlier and might prove to be too difficult to integrate into library instruction. However, there are examples of multiple-narrative transmedia that do meet the characteristics listed earlier. In these projects, the story can be experienced through distinctly separate media platforms, but all the platforms have been made accessible from a single entry point (e.g., a web site). Ruby Skye P.I. is an example of a multiple-narrative transmedia project. The central narrative is told through web episodes, with spin-off story elements available in the form of character weblogs and games. Ruby Skye P.I. was the project selected for the program example in this section. This program is equally suitable for school libraries or public libraries that offer library instruction to homeschoolers.

Program Example: Ruby Skye P. I.

Synopsis. Ruby Skye P. I. is a transmedia web series that follows the antics of teen detective, Ruby Skye, as she investigates and attempts to solve a variety of mysteries. From an e-mail scam to a missing will to a mysterious puppy, Ruby Skye P. I. engages viewers through a combination of action, comedy, and cliff-hangers. Beyond the web series, Ruby's story world includes her own Tumblr site, her sister Hailey's Tumblr site, the O'Deary Library page, the Friends of Needy Kids web site, and more. The games and puzzles introduced in the story can be played by viewers as well. All extensions of the story are accessible through the Ruby Skye P. I. web site.

Target Audience: Grades 5–8

Program Overview. This program example was designed for intermediate and middle school students. Seasons one and two of the Ruby Skye P. I. web series are used to enhance library instruction. Season one deals with the topic of e-mail scams, and serves as a springboard for teaching students how to identify Internet scams and hoaxes. Season two is centered on the O'Deary Library, which is used as an inspiration for a role-playing WebQuest that motivates students to practice their research skills.

Learning Activity 1: Scams and Hoaxes

Description. This activity uses the episodes from *The Spam Scam* to introduce students to the concept of scams and misinformation on the Internet. Ruby Skye finds out that her neighbor, Mrs. Gooje, has become the victim of an e-mail scam. Ruby solicits the help of her sister Hailey, and discovers that the scam e-mails can be traced back to her school's computers.

It is recommended that all 12 episodes of *The Spam Scam* be used for this activity. Altogether, viewing time takes approximately 50 minutes. This activity has been divided into four learning sessions, in which four episodes of *The Spam Scam* are viewed in each of the first three sessions, followed by discussion and a problem-solving exercise. The final session consists of a culminating project that allows each student to create a "Guide to Being Net Savvy" that can be posted in various places around the school or library.

Learning Objective(s):

- Understand the purpose of a scam or hoax.
- Identify the characteristics of a scam or hoax.
- Analyze a given web site or e-mail to determine its validity.
- Explain the characteristics that make a given web site or e-mail fictional or factual.

Materials and Equipment Needed:

- Ruby Skye P.I. web series (Season one; rubyskyepi.com)
- Computer, projector, screen, and speakers
- Computers, laptops, or tablets for students (Sessions 3 and 4)
- Internet access
- YouTube
- Microsoft Word or Google Docs
- Examples of e-mail and phishing scams, hoax web sites
- Rubric, if grading the activity
- One librarian

Step-by-Step Instructions:

Planning and Preparation

1. View *The Spam Scam* to become familiar with the story.
2. Find examples of e-mail and phishing scams, and hoax web sites to use in the sessions. (Sources: snopes.com, hoaxes.org)
3. If grading the culminating activity, create a rubric that can be shared with learners to set performance expectations.
4. Test equipment and web applications prior to the activity.

Implementation

Session 1:

1. Introduce the activity to students by asking: Have you ever been scammed? Do you know anyone who has been scammed?
2. Briefly introduce the Ruby Skye P.I. series, and then show the first four episodes (approximately 20 minutes)
3. After viewing the episodes, ask students: How did Ruby know that the e-mail was a scam?
4. Discuss the clues one might look for in identifying an e-mail scam. (5 minutes)

5. Present learners with handouts that include two examples of real-life e-mail scams.
6. Have learners work in pairs to:
   a. Highlight words and phrases in each example that might identify it as not real (e.g., misspelled words, too-good-to-be-true claims).
   b. Compare the two examples to find common clues and characteristics. (10–15 minutes)
7. As a whole group, have students discuss their findings and come up with a set of characteristics that can be used to determine if an e-mail is a scam. Record the characteristics for use in the last session. (5–10 minutes)

Session 2:

1. Show the second four episodes of *The Spam Scam*. (approximately 20 minutes)
2. After viewing the episodes, ask students: Phishing is another type of e-mail scam. Do you know what phishing means (spell out the word or write it on the board)?
3. Discuss the importance of not sharing personal information with unknown sources.
4. Discuss the clues one might look for in identifying a phishing scam. (5 minutes)
5. Present students with handouts that include two examples of real-life phishing scams. These often look legitimate on the surface.
6. Have students work in pairs to:
   a. Highlight words and phrases in each example that might identify it as not real (e.g., misspelled words, odd looking e-mail addresses, suspicious-looking files).
   b. Compare the two examples to find common clues and characteristics. (10–15 minutes)
7. As a whole group, have students discuss their findings and come up with a set of characteristics that can be used to determine a phishing scam. Add them to the class document for use in the last session. (5–10 minutes)

Session 3:
Note: Students will need computers, laptops, or tablets for this activity.

1. Show the last four episodes of *The Spam Scam*. (approximately 20 minutes)
2. After viewing the episodes, explain to students how web site hoaxes are similar to e-mail scams because they are fake.
3. Discuss the clues one might look for in identifying hoax web sites. Would the characteristics be similar to e-mail scams and phishing? (5 minutes)

4. Present each student with a web site and the task of determining whether it is real or hoax. Some students should receive real web sites, while others should receive hoax web sites.
5. Have students work in pairs to:
   a. Identify clues that help determine if the web site is real or fake. (each pair of students will work with two web sites)
   b. Write down their findings. (10–15 minutes)
6. As a whole group, have students discuss their findings and come up with an agreed-upon set of characteristics that can be used to determine the validity of a web site. Add them to the class document for use in the last session. (5–10 minutes)

Session 4:
Note: Students will need computers, laptops, or tablets for this activity.

1. Share handouts of the compiled findings and characteristics of scams and hoaxes that were recorded in Sessions 1–3.
2. Present students with the task of creating a Guide to Being Net Savvy in Word, Google Docs, or other software. The guide should demonstrate what they learned in Sessions 1–3.
3. Provide students with a rubric that communicates the performance expectations of the project.
4. Explain that the guides will be posted around the library or school (this should be motivating).
5. Encourage collaboration.

Learning Activity 2: Research Skills

Description. This activity uses the episodes from *The Haunted Library* as an inspiration for a role-playing WebQuest that hones learners' research skills. The owner of the O'Deary Library, Ava O'Deary, suddenly and mysteriously dies. She leaves behind a set of puzzles and clues that lead Ruby to her will.

It is recommended that all nine episodes of *The Haunted Library* be viewed as a part of this activity. Altogether, viewing time takes approximately 60 minutes. This activity has been divided into two learning sessions, in which the first seven episodes are viewed in the first session, leaving a cliff-hanger for the last two episodes to be viewed at the beginning of the second session. After viewing the last two episodes, learners will take part in a role-playing WebQuest that exercises their research skills.

Learning Objective(s):

- Given a research question, understand what information is needed to answer it.
- Use reasoning and logic to identify a resource that meets an information need.
- Using the identified resource, locate the needed information fluently.
- Communicate the answer to the research question clearly.

Materials and Equipment Needed:

- Ruby Skye P.I. web series (Season two; rubyskyepi.com)
- Computer, projector, screen, and speakers
- Computers, laptops, or tablets for learners (Session 2)
- Internet access
- YouTube
- WebQuest application, for example, Zunal (zunal.com)
- One librarian

Step-by-Step Instructions:

Planning and Preparation

1. View *The Haunted Library* to become familiar with the story.
2. Develop the Introduction and Task for the WebQuest. The Introduction situates learners in a role-playing scenario. The Task clearly describes the activity and the actions that the learners are expected to take.
3. For the Process section of the WebQuest, develop research questions that are drawn from the episodes.
4. It is recommended that a WebQuest application such as Zunal be used for this activity. However, WebQuests can be developed on any type of web-based platform.
5. Test equipment and web applications prior to the activity.
6. A sample WebQuest is included here.

Implementation

Session 1:

1. Briefly introduce the Ruby Skye P.I. series, and then show the first seven episodes of *The Haunted Library*. (approximately 50 minutes)
2. Inform students that the last two episodes will be viewed in the next session, followed by a WebQuest that will test their information-sleuthing skills.

Session 2:

Note: Students will need computers, laptops, or tablets for this activity.

1. Show the final two episodes of *The Haunted Library*. (approximately 15 minutes)
2. Introduce the WebQuest. Students can work in pairs.

WebQuest (sample)

Introduction:

You are the new librarian at the O'Deary Library. You have been left an enormous pile of work, including some reference questions that never got answered. It's time to think like a librarian! Are you up to the task?

Task:

Your first task as the new O'Deary Librarian is to tackle all the unanswered reference questions that have accumulated since Ophelia Bedelia was fired (she wasn't a very good librarian). There are six questions in total. As the new librarian, you want to show off your super librarian skills. To do that, you will need to meet the following expectations:

- Given a research question, understand what information is needed to answer it.
- Use reasoning and logic to identify a resource that meets an information need.
- Using the identified resource and locate the needed information fluently.
- Communicate the answer to the research question clearly.

Process:

You may work with a partner.

For the six reference questions given later in the chapter:

- Read each question carefully.
- Determine what information is needed to answer the question.
- From the sources provided, identify the one most likely to have the information you need. You may need to consult more than one information source to answer a question.
- Search the selected source efficiently to find the information you need. Use your sleuthing skills!
- Write down the answer(s) to each question. Provide the following information:

  □ Answer(s) to question
  □ Source(s) used (Don't cite Google, it's not a source)
  □ Source location(s)

Reference Question 1.

From Mrs. Googe: What exactly is a gherkin? How does it differ from a cucumber? Can you find me a good recipe for gherkins?

Reference Question 2.

From Diana: There's a book I want to read, but I don't know the name of it. It's blue. I think I saw Edmund reading it. What is the title of the book? Who is the author?

Reference Question 3.

From Ava (before she died): What is the difference between *Harry Potter and the Philosopher's Stone* and *Harry Potter and the Sorcerer's Stone*?

Reference Question 4.

From Ruby: What is fingerprint powder made out of? How does it work?

Reference Question 5.

From Henry O'Henry: What is the current exchange rate for 150 British pound sterling to US dollar?

Reference Question 6.

From Hailey: What are some good sources for information about girls' rights? I need library sources, like an article and a book.

Sources:
- Ruby Skye P. I.—rubyskyepi.com
- O'Deary Library—odearylibrary.com
- Student-friendly search engine (e.g., Kidtopia)
- Library databases, catalog

Evaluation:
If assessing the activity, include a rubric, survey, or quiz in this section.

Conclusion:
Being a librarian can be hard work. Some reference questions are more challenging than others. Not only do you have to figure out what kind of information is needed, you also need to know where to find it and how to find it quickly. Ruby Skye is good at putting clues together to solve mysteries. Finding answers to reference questions, like in this WebQuest, requires sleuthing too. Good information-sleuthing skills make research assignments easier and learning more fun!

Note to School Librarians: This program example was designed with middle-grade school librarians in mind. However, variations in scheduling may require modifications to the activities in order to make implementation feasible.

Learning Standards Alignments Include:

Common Core State Standards	Standards for the 21st-Century Learner	ISTE Standards for Students
CCSS.RI.6.6	1.1.7	1.a, 3.a, 3.b, 4.a, 4.c, 4.d. 5.b, 6.a
CCSS.RI.6.7	1.1.6, 1.1.7, 2.1.1, 2.1.3	1.a, 2.d, 3.a, 3.b, 3.c, 4.a, 4.c, 4.d. 5.b, 6.a
CCSS.W.6.2	2.1.6	1.a, 2.a, 2.b, 3.a, 3.b, 4.b, 5.b, 6.a, 6.b

Participatory Storytelling

Participatory storytelling is a collaborative process where members of a community come together to collectively create or contribute to a story. In one way or another, each participant in the community provides input that impacts the trajectory of the story line. Participatory storytelling can be game-like, allowing a community to vote on the direction of the story; or participatory storytelling can be creative, allowing a community to fully engage in the storytelling process, becoming the authors themselves of a collaboratively designed story world.

Different iterations of participatory storytelling include Twitter storytelling festivals, networked novels, and game-like participatory stories. A well-known example of a Twitter storytelling festival is the annual #TwitterFiction Festival, which showcases the talents of a diverse group of writers and performers. Stories in multiple genres unfold simultaneously during the event, with various media elements interwoven into the stories. An example of a networked novel is *Flight Paths* by Kate Pullinger, Chris Joseph, and participants. Pullinger and Joseph wrote and developed the transmedia storytelling project, integrating contributions from its readers that included new stories, personal narratives, and images. An example of a game-like participatory story on Tumblr is *Pigs vs. Wolf! You Decide Who Gets Eaten.* During the 30-minute time frame of the story, players were asked to tweet out their votes for the pigs or the wolf. Their votes changed the story's ending.

Participatory storytelling has its place among the traditional writing contests common in today's libraries, but potentially offers some advantages over those types of contests. First of all, participatory storytelling can serve as a more accessible entry point for those who wish to dabble in writing, but find a full writing contest intimidating. Unlike writing contests, in participatory storytelling, participants are not required to write a certain number of words. They can contribute as little or as much to the story as they wish. Second, participatory storytelling provides those who are new to writing an avenue to practice their craft among more expert writers. In that sense, participatory storytelling creates learning opportunities for fledgling writers. This may in fact lead to greater participation in libraries' traditional writing contests among individuals who got their feet wet through a participatory storytelling event. For some individuals, participatory storytelling programs may even be the spark needed to inspire a lifelong love of writing.

When planning for a participatory storytelling program or event, keep the following in mind: (1) the choice of participatory storytelling platform (e.g., Twitter, Tumblr, Instagram) should take into consideration what is already being widely used or available within the library community; (2) storytelling events should begin with a writing prompt that sets the theme and plot; (3) in addition to writing, participants should also be encouraged to contribute media elements to the story, such as art, sound, or animation; and (4) story writing guidelines should be clearly communicated (e.g., content, length limitations) and should be reflective of the library's Internet policies and procedures. The examples in this section offer guidance for planning and implementing two different types of participatory storytelling programs: a collaborative storytelling event using a social media platform, and a networked novel project inspired by Lewis Carroll's *Alice's Adventures in Wonderland*.

Program Example 1: Collaborative Storytelling Event

Target Audience. Young adults

Program Overview. This program example provides step-by-step instructions for planning and implementing a collaborative storytelling event similar to the #TwitterFiction Festival previously described. Guidelines for the program are written broadly, so that it may be adapted to a variety of social media platforms.

Materials and Equipment Needed:
- Social media platform (e.g., Twitter, Instagram, Pinterest, Facebook, Storify), considering the following:

- Platform should already be in use by the library
- Platform should already have a relatively good-sized following
- Platform should be well maintained by the library
- Platform should be moderately active, at a minimum
- Story writing prompt
- Participation rules, with clear guidelines on content and length
- Materials to market the event (e.g., posters, press release, newsletter, social media)
- Designated staff to facilitate the event, considering the following:
  - Social media platform needs to be managed during the entire length of the event.
  - If anticipating a high participation rate, two or more facilitators will be needed.
- Internet access
- Computers, laptops, or mobile devices

Step-by-Step Instructions:

Planning and Preparation

1. Identify the social media platform that will be used for the event.
2. Determine the length of the event. If sponsoring the event for the first time, consider a short time frame (e.g., 1–3 hours). If successful, subsequent events may be held over a longer period of time.
3. Create the story writing prompt. This will serve as the starting point for the entire storytelling event. If needed, use a plot generator (available on the web).
4. Develop the rules of participation for the event. These should be prominently displayed in any marketing materials, as well as on the event platform itself.
5. When drafting the rules, consider the following:
   a. To promote the creativity of impromptu storytelling, keep the story prompt a secret until the time of the event.
   b. Multiple threads will develop during the storytelling event. A hashtag is recommended to keep the story in one location.
   c. What is the duration of the event?
   d. Are there age restrictions?
   e. Are participants required to stick to the plot?
   f. What type of content is considered inappropriate?
   g. What is copyright appropriate? (e.g., images)
   h. Are there any limitations on length of text?
   i. Are there any limitations on media sharing?
6. Put together the marketing materials for the event.

7. To garner as much participation as possible, advertise the event well ahead of time, and through multiple media avenues.
8. Encourage library staff to participate in the event.
9. If the social media platform that is being used (e.g., Twitter) allows a feed to be embedded on a web site, consider embedding the storytelling feed on the library's home page just prior to the event.

Implementation
1. Release the storytelling prompt at the beginning of the event.
2. To get the ball rolling, begin by contributing to the storyline. Have other library staff do the same.
3. As the event gets underway, monitor for rogue contributions and delete or block only if necessary.
4. Consider using a tool like Storify to curate and share the storytelling event afterward.
5. If the storytelling event is particularly successful, consider partnering with area libraries in the future to create a larger collaborative storytelling festival.

Program Example 2: Networked Novel

Target Audience. All ages, or may be young adults

Program Overview. This program example provides step-by-step instructions for planning and implementing a networked novel project. The project takes an interactive fiction format. Given a detailed story beginning, participants can submit additions to the story at various points along the way. As a result, multiple submitted additions at each level branch out to create a nonlinear, "choose your own adventure" style of reading experience. The open-source tool, Twine, is used to create the networked novel. Participants submit their contributions to the project facilitator via e-mail or web-based form. The story is published in HTML, allowing it to be added to the library's web site. The theme for this example is Alice in Wonderland. A paragraph from a public domain edition of Lewis Carroll's *Alice's Adventures in Wonderland* is used as the storytelling prompt for the collaborative creation of newly imagined adventures for Alice.

Materials and Equipment Needed:
- Twine, open-source storytelling tool (twinery.org)
- Storytelling prompt

- Participation rules, with clear guidelines on content and length
- Materials to market the project (e.g., posters, press release, newsletter, social media)
- Designated staff to facilitate the project, considering the following:
  - Twine requires an understanding of HTML and/or wiki markup language
  - Story contributions will need to be submitted via e-mail or web-based form to the project facilitator, and should include the following information:
    - Submitter's name
    - Contact information
    - Text of story contribution
    - Images (optional)
    - Location in networked novel to place linked passage (citing the passage number should be sufficient)
- Internet access
- Computers, laptops, or mobile devices

Step-by-Step Instructions:

Planning and Preparation

1. Download Twine. Alternatively, it can be used online.
2. Learn how to use Twine. Wiki tutorials and a forum are available on the web site.
3. Determine the time frame of the project. A networked novel can be a long-term project, or be implemented over a shorter period of time. For this program example, the recommended time frame is a minimum of three months. That allows ample opportunity for participants to contribute enough to the project to make it a significant work of interactive fiction.
4. In Twine, develop the Starting Point page for the project. Include the following:
   a. An introduction that describes the purpose and goal of the project.
   b. Rules for participation in the project, with guidelines on content and length of contributions. Content should be appropriate for all ages and stick to the theme of the story (in this case, Further Adventures of Alice). It is recommended that contributions be limited to no more than 250 words each.
   c. Directions for submitting story contributions. A web-based form is recommended to ensure that adequate information is included for proper placement in the story.
5. Create a passage for the beginning storytelling prompt:
   a. "'Oh, I've had such a curious dream!' said Alice, and she told her sister, as well as she could remember them, all these strange Adventures of

hers that you have just been reading about; and when she had finished, her sister kissed her, and said, 'It was a curious dream, dear, certainly: but now run in to your tea; it's getting late.' So Alice got up and ran off, thinking while she ran, as well she might, what a wonderful dream it had been." (Chapter XII. Alice's Evidence. Project Gutenberg edition)

   b. This will serve as the first passage in the story.

   c. Label this passage with a Roman numeral I.

   d. Link this page to the Starting Point page in Twine.

6. Put together the marketing materials for the project.

7. In addition to marketing the project, consider offering several brief sessions prior to the project launch to explain it further, and demonstrate what it will look like.

8. Encourage library staff to participate in the project.

Implementation

1. To launch the project, publish the file (HTML), and add it to the library's web site. Be sure to create a prominent link to it on the library's home page so that it can be easily found.

2. As new passage contributions come in, add them to the story by linking them from the previous passage as indicated by the participant.

3. Label each new passage link with a number to make them easier to manage. The text box below provides a visual example of what the story structure looks like in Twine:

I. 'Oh, I've had such a curious dream!' said Alice, and she told her sister, as well as she could remember them, all these strange Adventures of hers that you have just been reading about; and when she had finished, her sister kissed her, and said, 'It was a curious dream, dear, certainly: but now run in to your tea; it's getting late.' So Alice got up and ran off, thinking while she ran, as well she might, what a wonderful dream it had been.
What did Alice dream?

Ia. The Pink Rabbit
Ib. Back Down the Rabbit Hole
Ic. The Jolly Jabberwocky

---

4. As each contribution gets added, republish the file so that it will appear online.

5. The growing project should adhere to the following format:

a. Each passage should be numbered according to its location in the story, as seen in Step 3. This way, participants are able to indicate the passage number from which they would like to link their new contribution.

b. Each page within Twine will contain a single passage, plus links to the next part of the story.

c. Numerous links might follow each passage. Each link indicates an alternative storyline (i.e., choose your own adventure).

d. Each link should be titled in a way that describes the passage it links to, allowing readers to choose the path that they find most intriguing.

e. The completed project will be a work of interactive fiction that encompasses many different story paths and endings.

6. When the project wraps up, remove the rules of participation from the Starting Point Page. The storytelling prompt page will become the new Starting Point Page.

7. If the project is successful, consider turning it into an ongoing program.

8. Completed projects can become a part of the library's interactive fiction collection.

Note to School Librarians: Both of the participatory storytelling program examples have the potential to be modified as collaborative school-wide learning projects that promote multimodal literacy development. For example, a networked novel program at the school-wide (or even district-wide) level might serve as an alternative to a one-book program—that is, students would actively contribute to the writing of a novel rather than just reading one.

Learning Standards Alignments Include:

Common Core State Standards	Standards for the 21st-Century Learner	ISTE Standards for Students
CCSS.CCRA.W.3	3.1.3	1.a, 1.b, 2.a, 2.b, 3.a, 3.b, 4.a, 4.b, 4.d, 5.b, 6.a, 6.b, 6.c
CCSS.CCRA.W.4	2.1.2	2.b, 3.b, 4.b, 6.b
CCSS.CCRA.W.6	3.1.2, 3.1.3, 3.1.4	1.a, 1.b, 1.c, 2.a, 2.b, 3.a, 3.b, 4.a, 4.b, 4.d, 5.b, 6.a, 6.b, 6.c
CCSS.CCRA.W.8	1.1.1, 1.3.3	1.a, 3.a, 3.b, 3.c, 3.d, 4.a, 4.b, 4.c,4.d, 5.a, 6.b

Transmedia Gaming Event

Transmedia gaming events are community-wide campaigns that are typically based on the concept of alternate reality games. They utilize multiple media platforms to deliver both narrative and gaming elements. Some even encourage collaboration among players to solve clues. All transmedia gaming events share the goal of immersing participants in a storytelling experience that blends reality with fantasy.

Outside the library world, transmedia gaming events have proven to be popular marketing tools for branding campaigns that strive to extend their message to consumers through a storytelling experience. For example, in 2013, Chipotle ran a transmedia branding campaign that involved an animation short about a scarecrow living in a dystopian world overrun by processed foods. To extend that storyline, a game app was created for consumers to download so that they could continue participating in the storytelling experience.

Another example is the *I Love Bees* transmedia campaign that served as publicity for the debut of Microsoft's *Halo 2* video game. *I Love Bees* was an alternate reality game developed by game design company 42 Entertainment that showed up as a hidden URL in the *Halo 2* trailer. The web site, ilovebees.com, served as the starting point for the game, and was narrated by a girl named Dana Awbrey, who had built the *I Love Bees* web site for her Aunt Margaret. Dana was seeking out help to figure out what happened to the web site. It had been hacked in a disturbing way, and her mother's e-mail had been hijacked. The game took players through multiple platforms to gather clues—from the web site, to Dana's weblog, to GPS coordinates and pay phones. In the end, players had to use collective intelligence to solve the clues and win the game (McGonigal 2008).

Libraries can develop transmedia gaming events that not only serve as publicity tools but also as community building programs that bring current library users and newcomers together in a shared storytelling experience. The programs need not be as complex as the examples illustrated previously though. However, all library-based transmedia gaming events should include the following five basic elements: (1) a well-developed and intriguing library-centric story that serves as the starting point for the game, (2) a blend of realistic and fantastical elements in the storyline, (3) multiple platforms for telling the story and dispensing clues; (4) a gathering place for collecting clues that encourages collaboration among players, and (5) a game master who can tailor the trajectory of the game to its situational dynamics. The program example in this section illustrates how all five of those elements can come together to create a library-based transmedia gaming event.

Program Example: "The Book Worm"

Story: The library catalog has been infected with the dreaded Book Worm virus! The Book Worm virus first infects a system by attaching itself to a single item record. The trouble happens when that item gets checked out. Then, the Book Worm virus begins to replicate and attach itself to other records. Eventually, the entire catalog system becomes so infected that all records are lost! To prevent that from happening, the mission is to find out which record contains the Book Worm virus and clean it up before that item gets checked out. Antivirus software can only go so far in identifying the location of the virus. It takes days to run the antivirus software through the entire system and it is only capable of providing numerical data output that must be converted to something more meaningful and pieced together to solve the problem of the virus's location. The library community must now come together to help solve the case of the elusive Book Worm virus!

Target Audience: All ages

Program Overview: This program example shows how a simple story can become the starting point for a transmedia gaming event that brings library community members together to solve clues and save the library from the dreaded Book Worm virus. Step-by-step instructions are provided for planning and implementing the program. Multiple media platforms are used to implement the game. The length of the gaming event is determined by the quickness of its participants in solving clues.

Materials and Equipment Needed:
- Media platforms for dispensing clues and communicating with players, for example, social media, e-mail, library web site, weblog
- Library item and its "infected" record; choose an item that gets checked out infrequently to ensure opportunity for gameplay
- Large bulletin board or whiteboard to serve as a central location for gathering clues
- Descriptive signage for bulletin board or whiteboard
- One library staff member to serve as game master
- Resource to convert text to numbers, such as unit-conversion.info

Step-by-Step Instructions:
Planning and Preparation
1. Determine a time for holding the event. Be sure to take into consideration how it will be impacted by other major library activities that are occurring at the same time. For example, if the event is to take place over the

summer, might it draw more participants or might it get lost among various other summer library activities?

2. Once the event has been scheduled, identify the library item(s) and record(s) that will be used as part of the game.

3. For each item chosen, select four to five elements from its catalog record that can be expressed in numerical format (i.e., words that can be converted to numbers or number elements from the record). These elements will function as individual clues and should be relatively difficult to decipher on their own, but together should create a fairly clear picture of the location of the "infected" record(s). For example, for the title, *The World According to Garp*, the following clues might be used:

   a. Binary code: 01110111 01101111 01110010 01101100 01100100 (translate: world)

   b. ASCII: 097 099 099 111 114 100 105 110 103 (translate: according)

   c. Hexadecimal: 67 61 72 70 (translate: Garp)

   d. ISBN: 9780525237709 (could work as the final clue)

4. Identify the time frame and the order in which the clues will be dispensed. For example, clues might be dispensed in order of most difficult to easiest.

5. Set up the whiteboard or bulletin board in a location that is heavily trafficked. Signage should be added after the game begins.

6. Create an outline of the game plan to provide to all library staff. In order to create an alternate reality game environment, library staff will need to play their part in the storyline.

7. Identify the best avenues for communicating clues to the library community. Clues should be shared daily through multiple outlets. They should also be posted on the designated bulletin board in the library every morning during the gaming event.

8. Create a message (i.e., plea of help) to send out to the library community on the first day of the gaming event. This should be sent through the library's social media outlets. Also, consider posting the message prominently on the library's web site. The message should look something like this:

   a. ATTENTION LIBRARY PATRONS: The staff at [Name of Library] desperately needs your help! Our library catalog has been infected with the dreaded Book Worm virus! Right now, it is hiding in one of the catalog records. If the item attached to that record gets checked out, the Book Worm will be activated and spread into other records. To prevent this from happening, we need to find the infected record right away! We have a problem though—our antivirus software is only capable of providing us with numerical data from the infected record. So, we are asking for your help to figure out what these data mean so that we can find the location of the Book Worm virus before it spreads!

9. Keep in mind that the blending of fantasy and reality in this type of gaming event might confuse some library users at first.

Implementation

1. On the first day of the gaming event, post the plea of help across the library's multiple media outlets, ideally including the library's web site.
2. If not previously managed, set up the bulletin board or white board with signage.
3. Post the first clue(s) through the library's selected media outlets, as well as on the bulletin board.
4. It is likely that the object of the game will need to be further explained to library users in the beginning of the event. However, to keep the alternate reality elements authentic to the game, try to maintain a role-playing atmosphere when doing so.
5. Continue to post new clues each day.
6. The game master should keep tabs on the players' progress, and add additional clues if necessary.
7. As an additional clue, the "infected" catalog record can also be subtly modified as the game progresses (e.g., slowly removing bits and pieces from the record's title and author).
8. Once the item is found, the game ends. However, if the item gets checked out prior to identifying the first "infected" record then the game can continue. In that case, the storyline should continue with another "infected" record and item (meaning the Book Worm replicated). It is up to the game master to decide how long the game will go on for, and how difficult it will be!

Note to School Librarians: A transmedia gaming event of this scale may not be feasible in a school library. However, on a smaller scale the gaming event can be modified into an activity that introduces students to research and technology skills through gamification. As students combine clues and search the catalog in an effort to identify the "infected" record, they are performing inquiry-based searching to solve a problem.

Transmedia Technology Planning

Phase One: Assess ■ Phase Two: Set Goals ■ Phase Three: Identify Technology Resources ■ Phase Four: Create an Action Plan ■ Phase Five: Evaluate and Revise

Transmedia storytelling encompasses technology-rich resources that may run on a variety of hardware and software platforms. When integrating such sources into library programming, additional technology tools are often utilized to enhance the participatory experience of library users. For example, the maker program in Chapter Five not only employed the transmedia storytelling project *Inanimate Alice* but it also required the use of digital creation tools, such as Storybird and Scratch. Consequently, such a program would require careful technology planning.

The objective of this chapter is to outline the process of technology planning for transmedia storytelling programs in libraries. Transmedia technology planning should be viewed as an iterative process that encompasses five phases as shown in Figure 6.1. It should be noted that the planning process discussed in this chapter was written with public libraries in mind. However, it may be possible to adapt the process to school libraries in the context of planning collaborative cross-curricular programs (e.g., STEAM curriculum).

Assessing the needs and interests of the library community and the limitations of library technology characterizes the first phase of the transmedia technology planning process. This phase is undertaken in an effort to determine the types of transmedia storytelling programs that will best serve the library community.

Figure 6.1 Technology planning process for transmedia programs.

The library community includes library users, potential library users, partnering organizations (e.g., public schools), library staff, administration, and trustees. Needs, interests, and limitations may be assessed in a number of ways, including observation, conversation, surveys, and resource inventory.

Setting goals for transmedia programming characterizes the next phase in the technology planning process. Programming goals are developed to align with the library community's needs, interests, and limitations as assessed in the first phase. Goals describe the type of program, its purpose, the target audience, and the expected program outcome. Program outcomes reflect the library's mission, vision, and/or values statements.

The third phase in the transmedia technology planning process entails the identification of potential technology resources for each programming goal. Technology resources include equipment and software applications required for each library program, as well as the identification of potential technology resources that the library may wish to acquire to meet a programming goal. If needed, budgetary matters for hardware or software should be addressed at this time as well.

The fourth phase in the transmedia technology planning process involves the development of an action plan for each of the transmedia programming goals. This phase synthesizes the results of the first three phases in the technology planning process. Goals, tasks, technology resources, time frames, and program evaluation methods are charted out for the purpose of creating a guide to program implementation. Technology training needs are also identified in this phase. Such documentation is especially beneficial for transmedia programs that require the involvement of multiple staff.

The fifth phase of the transmedia technology planning process is evaluation. In this phase, the action plan is examined to determine if any additional information is required before program implementation begins. Once a working action plan is in place, periodical evaluation is recommended to update and revise as needed.

Because transmedia library programs run the gamut from transmedia fiction clubs to transmedia story times and from interactive displays to maker programs, multiple staff involvement is essential. For that reason, it is recommended that the transmedia technology planning process include a committee of staff members representing different aspects of the library programs and services that transmedia storytelling enhances. For example, a committee might consist of a children's librarian, a youth librarian, a programming librarian, and a technology librarian (or IT staff member).

The sections that follow take a closer look at each phase of the transmedia technology planning process and include:

- Guiding questions
- Templates
- Examples

Phase One: Assess

Assessing the needs of the library community requires the input of multiple groups. Each group has different interests that should be taken into consideration when determining the type of transmedia storytelling programs to offer in the library. In addition to the library community, library technology needs to be assessed as part of the transmedia technology planning process. Transmedia library programs are heavily dependent on the use of technology, and technology limitations should be considered when planning library programs centered on transmedia storytelling.

The following two tables provide guiding questions for the assessment phase. Table 6.1 provides guiding questions for assessing various library groups. Table 6.2 provides guiding questions for assessing library technology resources. Guiding questions can be used to make observations, create resource inventories, pose informal inquiries, or even develop more formal surveys in the assessment phase of the transmedia technology planning process.

Table 6.1: Guiding Questions for Assessing Library Community Groups

Library Group	Guiding Questions
Library Users	• What are the demographics of your library users? • Do the demographics of your library users reflect the demographics of the larger community the library serves? Are any demographics missing in that picture? • Are there specific needs among certain library users that are not being met? (e.g., early literacy activities, digital literacy skills) • Are you aware of specific interests among certain library users that are not being met? (e.g., gaming, coding) • How do library users currently interact with the library? (e.g., check social media, study) • How could library users better interact with the library? • Which current library program offerings have been most popular? • Have library users requested specific types of programs? • Do any informal hobby groups meet regularly in your library? (e.g., writers' groups, fan clubs)
Potential Library Users	• Has the library ever offered events to attract new library users? • How does the library interact with the larger community it serves? (e.g., social media, newsletters) • Does the library strive to offer a variety of programs to attract a wide range of demographic groups? • Does the library participate in any outreach services that might connect potential library users to library resources and program offerings?
Partnering Organizations (e.g., public schools, after-school programs, adult literacy groups, early literacy groups)	• What community organizations does the library work with? • Has the library ever partnered with the local school(s) to provide library instruction to learners? • Does the library offer field trip tours for local schoolchildren? • Does the library sponsor any after-school programs for specific organizations? (e.g., 4-H, Girl Scouts) • Has the library ever partnered with local preschools to provide early literacy activities? • Does the library partner with adult literacy organizations? • What opportunities exist within the community for the library to create new partnerships with local organizations?

Library Staff	• How many staff members are currently involved in library program development?
	• Does the library have a full-time librarian or staff member solely dedicated to programming?
	• Does the library have a children's librarian?
	• Does the library have a youth librarian?
	• Have any collaborative programming efforts been made across different departments within the library? (e.g., digital literacy in early childhood)
	• How many staff members consider themselves technologically savvy, or at least comfortable with technology?
Administrators or Library Trustees	• Is technology viewed as a critical component of library services?
	• Does the library's mission, vision, or values statement emphasize its role in 21st-century learning? (e.g., lifelong learning, digital literacy, information literacy)
	• Is innovative library programming supported? (e.g., makerspaces)

Table 6.2: Guiding Questions for Assessing Library Technology

Library Technology	Guiding Questions
Audiovisual Equipment	• Does the library own an AV projector and screen? Is the projector and screen readily available for library programs? Is the projector and screen mobile?
	• Does the library own a set of microphones? Are the microphones readily available for library programs?
	• Does the library lend headphones to library users? How many headphone sets does the library own? Are headphones available for library programs if needed?
Computers and Laptops	• Does the library have a computer lab or other space available for programs that require computer access? How many computers are available for that purpose?
	• Does the library make laptops available for programs that require them? How many laptops can be used for that purpose?
Mobile Technology	• Does the library own tablets that can be used in programs? How many tablets does the library own?
	• What other mobile devices does the library own?
Other Technologies	• Does the library own a touch screen TV? Is it available for use in programs or interactive displays?
	• Does the library own an interactive whiteboard? Is it portable?

(Continued)

Table 6.2: Continued

Library Technology	Guiding Questions
Software Applications	• Does the library curate or provide easy access to digital creation tools for library users? (e.g., Scratch, Storybird, Mozilla Webmaker) • Does the library provide access to applications on both computer and tablet? • Do security barriers exist for downloading free applications on computers and tablets? (e.g., Scratch) • Are IT requests for downloading free applications met in a timely manner? • What software licenses or subscriptions has the library purchased? (e.g., Microsoft Office, Adobe InDesign, Camtasia)
Internet Access	• Is Internet access reliable in the library? • Is Wi-Fi available in all areas of the library? Is Wi-Fi reliable?

Phase Two: Set Goals

Phase two entails setting transmedia programming goals based on the findings from the needs assessment in phase one. Results from phase one should provide adequate insight into the various needs and interests of the library community, as well any programming gaps that transmedia storytelling might fill. Additionally, the policy and technology parameters identified in phase one should inform the transmedia technology planning process.

Goal setting provides clear direction for the planning process. Because multiple parties are likely to be involved in both transmedia storytelling program planning and implementation, clearly defined and agreed-upon programming goals will make the process run more smoothly. Transmedia programming goals should be written in a way that fully communicates the following information:

- Type of transmedia program (e.g., story time, maker program, gaming event)
- Target audience
- Purpose of the program
- Expected outcome
- Reflection of the library's mission, vision, or values statements

Table 6.3 provides examples of programming goals for each transmedia storytelling program type presented in Chapter Five.

Table 6.3: Examples of Transmedia Programming Goals

Program Type	Example Programming Goal
Transmedia Story Time	A transmedia story time program for preschoolers will be developed to enhance early literacy through the evidence-based practice of interactive storytelling. Transmedia elements will serve the purpose of creating an environment that encourages and enables children to actively participate in the storytelling process, fostering language and literacy development through interactive role-play.
Transmedia-Inspired Maker Program	A maker program inspired by the world of transmedia storytelling will be developed to engage preteens in design thinking projects (e.g., digital storytelling, game making). Transmedia elements from the selected story will serve as models for constructing new iterations of the story, requiring participants to exercise critical-thinking and problem-solving skills as they design their digital creations.
Interactive Library Display	An interactive library display will be developed for all library users with the purpose of motivating a curiosity for lifelong learning. Transmedia storytelling will serve as the central narrative in the display. All display materials will function as separate entry points into the themes of the story, enabling deeper exploration and creating the conditions necessary for lifelong learning to take place.
Transmedia Gaming Event	A transmedia gaming event will be created to serve as a publicity tool for the library. The game will be conducted through multiple outlets (e.g., social media, e-mail, web site, library) to capture the intrigue of both regular library users and potential new library users. The game will be set up to encourage collaborative problem solving.
Transmedia Fiction Club	A transmedia fiction club will be started for young adults to explore the story connections of popular multiple-narrative transmedia franchises (e.g., Hunger Games, Game of Thrones). Participants will be invited to discuss their perspectives as they experience each story realm (e.g., novel, movie, game).
Transmedia-Inspired Library Instruction	Partnering with the local public schools, an information literacy program will be developed to address K-12 learners' library research and technology skills. Transmedia storytelling will serve as the impetus for the program, with a story-based instructional approach that motivates and engages learners in learning. In addition to public school learners, homeschooled learners will be invited to participate in the program.

(Continued)

Table 6.3: Continued

Program Type	Example Programming Goal
Participatory Storytelling Program	A participatory storytelling program will be developed to engage library users of all ages in creative writing endeavors. The program will construct an environment that allows budding writers of all ages to exercise their imaginations as they collectively contribute to a transmedia story project. The finished story project will become a permanent part of the library's collection.

Phase Three: Identify Technology Resources

Phase three involves identifying the types of technologies most suited to each of the transmedia programming goals developed during phase two. Phase three should be considered a brainstorming activity. All of the library's existing (and potential) technologies that match each programming goal should be identified and cataloged in a chart. The chart that is constructed in this phase will serve as a resource for the final selection of program technologies when creating an action plan in phase four. The chart also provides working documentation for long-range planning of any future transmedia storytelling programs.

Table 6.4 provides a model of how a library's technologies can be charted to each of the example programming goals from Table 6.3 in the previous section. Appendices A and B list additional transmedia storytelling resources and technology tools.

Phase Four: Create an Action Plan

In phase four, all of the accumulated work from the previous three phases comes together to produce an action plan for *each* programming goal set forth by the transmedia technology planning committee. The technology resources identified in phase three provide a basis for mapping out the objectives and tasks (including training) that are needed to reach each programming goal. Because this chapter is focused on technology planning, it must be noted that the central purpose of the action plan is for technology decision making and delivery. Other areas of program planning, such as publicity, are outside the scope of this chapter.

Table 6.5 provides a sample action plan for the transmedia-inspired maker program example from phase two of the technology planning process. It is important to remember that each transmedia storytelling program will require the development of a separate action plan.

Table 6.4: Example Programming Goals with Potential Technology Resources

Example Programming Goal	Transmedia	Technology Resources	
		Software	Hardware
A transmedia story time program for preschoolers will be developed to enhance early literacy through the evidence-based practice of interactive storytelling. Transmedia elements will serve the purpose of creating an environment that encourages and enables children to actively participate in the storytelling process, fostering language and literacy development through interactive role-play.	*Rockford's Rock Opera* PBS KIDS (e.g., *Curious George, Cat in the Hat*) Nick Jr. (e.g., *Max and Ruby, Peter Rabbit*) Disney Junior (e.g., *Doc McStuffins*)	Internet browser with Flash plug-in	Overhead projector Projector screen Computers or laptops Tablets Microphones Interactive whiteboard Touchscreen TV
A maker program inspired by the world of transmedia storytelling will be developed to engage preteens in design thinking projects (e.g., digital storytelling, game making). Transmedia elements from the selected story will serve as models for constructing new iterations of the story, requiring participants to exercise critical thinking and problem-solving skills as they design their digital creations.	*Rockford's Rock Opera Inanimate Alice Robot Heart Stories Star Wars*	Internet browser with Flash and/or Unity plug-in Storybird Mozilla Webmaker ThingLink, Scratch Animoto LEGO Movie Maker	Computers or laptops Tablets 3-D printer
An interactive library display will be developed for all library users with the purpose of motivating a curiosity for lifelong learning. Transmedia storytelling will serve as the central narrative in the	*Rockford's Rock Opera Circa 1948* Lord of the Rings	Internet browser with Flash and/or Unity plug-in Library databases(s)	Computers Tablets Touch screen TV

(Continued)

Example Programming Goal	Technology Resources		
	Transmedia	Software	Hardware
display. All display materials will function as separate entry points into the themes of the story, enabling deeper exploration and creating the conditions necessary for lifelong learning to take place.	*Collapsus*	Animoto LEGO Movie Maker	Interactive whiteboard
An original transmedia gaming event will be created to serve as a publicity tool for the library. The game will be conducted through multiple outlets (e.g., social media, e-mail, web site, library) to capture the intrigue of both regular library users and potential new library users. The game will be set up to encourage collaborative problem solving.		Social media tools Weblog platform Library web site Library catalog Library database(s)	Computers Tablets Touch screen TV Interactive whiteboard
A transmedia fiction club will be started for young adults to explore both single-narrative and multiple-narrative transmedia. Participants will discuss how each media element in a given transmedia piece contributes to the overall storytelling experience.	The Lizzie Bennet Diaries 39 Clues Gone Home Green Gables Fables	Internet browser with Flash and/or Unity plug-in YouTube	Projector Screen Computers or laptops Tablets Microphones Interactive whiteboard Game console

Description	Titles	Software	Hardware
Partnering with the local public schools, an information literacy program will be developed to address K-12 learners' library research and technology skills. Transmedia storytelling will serve as the impetus for the program, with a story-based instructional approach that motivates and engages learners in learning. In addition to public school learners, homeschooled learners will be invited to participate in the program as well.	*Inanimate Alice* *Rockford's Rock Opera* <u>Ruby Skye P.I.</u>	Internet browser with Flash and/or Unity plug-in Library databases(s) Storybird Mozilla Webmaker ThingLink Screencast-o-matic Scratch	Overhead projector Projector screen Computers or laptops Microphones Interactive whiteboard
A participatory storytelling program will be developed to engage library users of all ages in creative writing endeavors. The program will construct an environment that allows budding writers of all ages to exercise their imaginations as they collectively contribute to a transmedia story project. The finished story project will become a permanent part of the library's collection.		Twine Social media tools Weblog platform Library web site Embeddable polling software	Computers or laptops Tablets Touchscreen TV Interactive whiteboard

Table 6.5: Sample Action Plan for the Transmedia Technology Planning Process

Example Programming Goal:

A maker program inspired by the world of transmedia storytelling will be developed to engage preteens in design thinking projects (e.g., digital storytelling, game making). Transmedia elements from the selected story will serve as models for constructing new iterations of the story, requiring participants to exercise critical-thinking and problem-solving skills as they design their digital creations.

Objectives	Tasks	Time	Resources
Select an engaging transmedia story that will appeal to the library's target preteen audience.	✓ Read or "play" through each transmedia story option. ✓ Look for stories with themes and/or characters that are relevant to the target audience. ✓ Use the library's selection policy as an additional guideline. ✓ Choose two to three story options and have the programming committee vote on the final selection.	One to two weeks	Use the resource documentation that was developed in phase three of the transmedia technology planning process. See Table 6.4 for example.
Choose three to four maker activities that fit well with the characteristics of the selected transmedia story.	✓ Research what has already been done with the selected transmedia story in terms of maker activities. ✓ Gather additional ideas from maker activity resource guides. ✓ Choose maker activities that will allow the audience to expand the story world through character(s), theme(s), or media elements.	One to two weeks	✓ Research on selected transmedia story ✓ *Make* magazine ✓ Maker Education Initiative
Select the technology tool(s) that will be used for the maker activities.	✓ Choose technology tool(s) that will help the audience achieve the project goals of each maker activity. ✓ Choose technology tool(s) that are appropriate for both age and ability. ✓ Include library staff who will be working with the tools in the decision-making process.	One to two weeks	Use the resource documentation that was developed in phase three of the transmedia technology planning process. See Table 6.4 for example.
Select the hardware devices that will be used for the maker activities.	✓ Choose the hardware devices or equipment that best meets the project goals of each maker activity. ✓ Choose hardware devices that work in conjunction with technology tools.	One to two weeks	Use the resource documentation that was developed in phase three of the transmedia technology planning process. See Table 6.4 for example.

Task	Timeframe	Details	Resources
Install, download, or provide access to the technology tools on the devices that will be used for the maker activities.	One to two weeks	✓ Request IT staff assistance, if needed, for technology applications that require installation or download (e.g., open-source software, proprietary software). ✓ Request web maintenance staff assistance, if needed, to make browser-based applications easily accessible from the library's web site. ✓ Test all technology applications to ensure smooth operation.	One to two IT staff, web maintenance staff
Train programming staff on the use of the selected technology applications and devices.	Ongoing	✓ Offer training sessions on technology applications and devices to any programming staff who will be involved in the maker program. ✓ Provide access to online tutorials for selected technology applications and hardware devices for easy staff and library user reference.	Tutorials usually available within technology application sites. Also, try: ✓ YouTube ✓ Atomic Learning (subscription) ✓ Lynda.com (subscription)
Create example projects for each of the maker activities.	One to two weeks	Creating example projects: ✓ Provides sample materials for publicizing the maker program. ✓ Provides the maker program audience with a sample end product. ✓ Provides the programming staff ample opportunity to genuinely learn the technology applications, so that expert guidance can be given as needed during the maker activities.	✓ Transmedia story selection ✓ Selected technology applications ✓ Creativity and imagination
Create digital badges (if using) to reflect maker project accomplishments.	One week	✓ Creating digital badges that can be earned for each maker activity project is optional. ✓ If used, digital badges can be displayed on a web page that is devoted to the library's maker program.	✓ Credly ✓ Open Badge Designer

Phase Five: Evaluate and Revise

The final phase in the transmedia technology planning process is evaluating and revising all aspects of the technology planning process. Evaluation helps to determine if any changes need to be made prior to beginning the implementation process of the transmedia storytelling programs. Once the technology plans are put into action, it should be expected that minor revisions will need to be made. However, careful technology planning will result in a much smoother process. Table 6.6 provides guiding questions that will aid in evaluating the transmedia technology planning process.

Table 6.6: Guiding Questions for the Evaluating and Revising Phase

Programming Goals (evaluate each goal separately)	• Does the programming goal fill an unmet *need* in the library community?
	• Does the programming goal fill an unmet *interest* in the library community?
	• Will the programming goal attract an underserved demographic in the library community?
	• Does the programming goal appeal to a broad range of abilities?
	• Is sufficient library staff available to meet the programming goal?
	• Does the programming goal work within the parameters of the library's technology capabilities?
	• Does the programming goal reflect the library's mission, vision, or values statements?
Technology Resources	• Was the planning committee able to identify adequate technology resource choices to match programming goals?
	• Does the library have all the technology resources necessary for meeting programming goals?
	• Will the library be able to acquire all the technology resources necessary to meet programming goals?
Action Plan	• Do the objectives help meet the programming goals?
	• Are any objectives missing in the action plan?
	• Do the identified tasks adequately meet each objective in the action plan?
	• Are any tasks missing in the action plan?
	• Is the time frame sufficient for the transmedia technology planning process?
	• Did the technology resource document provide adequate choices in the action planning process?

Transmedia
Storytelling Resources

The following list of transmedia storytelling resources is organized by title and genre, and includes the projects that were discussed in this book, as well as additional transmedia storytelling projects that librarians may find useful as resources.

Title	Genre	Available from
39 Clues	Franchise	the39clues.scholastic.com
Aesop's Fables	Interactive fiction	penguin.com/static/ packages/us/yreaders/ aesop/
Autobiography of Jane Eyre	Web series	theautobiographyofja.wix .com/jane-eyre
Beneath Floes	Interactive fiction	bravemule.com/ beneathfloes
Circa 1948	Interactive fiction	circa1948.nfb.ca
Clifford the Big Red Dog	Franchise	teacher.scholastic.com/ clifford1
Cloud Chamber	Transmedia game	cloudchambermystery .com
Collapsus	Transmedia game	collapsus.com
Depression Quest	Transmedia game	depressionquest.com
Emma Approved	Web series	pemberleydigital.com/ emma-approved
Endgame by James Frey	Franchise	endgameiscoming.com

Title	Genre	Available from
Ever, Jane	Transmedia game	everjane.com
Flight Paths	Networked novel	flightpaths.net
Frankenstein MD	Web series	pemberleydigital.com/ frankenstein-md
Fury of Solace	Web series	furyofsolace.com
Gone Home	Transmedia game	gonehomegame.com
Green Gables Fables	Web series	greengablesfables.com
Inanimate Alice	Interactive fiction	inanimatealice.com
Infinity Ring by James Dashner	Franchise	infinityring.scholastic .com
The Lizzie Bennet Diaries	Web series	pemberleydigital.com/ the-lizzie-bennet-diaries
Lord of the Rings Online (game)	Franchise	lotro.com
Lowlifes	Interactive fiction	zenfilms.com/lowlifes
March Family Letters	Web series	pemberleydigital.com/ the-march-family-letters
Minecraft (game)	Franchise	minecraft.net
Never Alone	Transmedia game	neveralonegame.com
Nick Jr.	Franchise	nickjr.com
PBS KIDS	Franchise	pbskids.org
Pottermore (game)	Franchise	pottermore.com
Robot Heart Stories	Participatory project	robotsjourney.tumblr.com
Rockford's Rock Opera	Interactive fiction	rockfordsrockopera.com
Ruby Skye P.I.	Web series	rubyskyepi.com
Seven Digital Deadly Sins	Interactive documentary	sins.nfb.ca/#/Home
Skeleton Creek by Patrick Carman	Franchise	patrickcarman.com/enter/ skeleton-creek
Spirit Animals by Brandon Mull	Franchise	spiritanimals.scholastic .com
TombQuest by Michael Northrop	Franchise	tombquest.scholastic.com
Warrior Cats by Erin Hunter	Franchise	warriorcats.com
Welcome to Pinepoint	Interactive documentary	pinepoint.nfb.ca/#/ pinepoint
Welcome to Sanditon	Web series	pemberleydigital.com/ welcome-to-sanditon

APPENDIX B

Technology Tools

The technology tools listed in this appendix are especially useful for the participatory activities that accompany transmedia storytelling programs (e.g., maker activities). With the exception of social media platforms, all of the digital creation tools mentioned in Chapters Five and Six, as well as additional useful tools, are included in this list.

Tool	Description	Available from
Animoto	Video-making tool	animoto.com
Audacity	Free multitrack audio editor and recorder	audacity.sourceforge.net
Camtasia	Screen recorder and video editor	techsmith.com/camtasia
Canva	Graphic design software; iOS app available	canva.com
Conducttr	Transmedia storytelling software	conducttr.com
Credly	Digital badge creator	credly.com
GameMaker: Studio	Game development software	yoyogames.com/studio
GoAnimate	Animated video maker	goanimate.com
Haiku Deck	Presentation software; iOS app available	haikudeck.com
iMotion	Stop-motion app for iOS	fingerlab.net
Issuu	Digital publishing platform	issuu.com
Jing	Free screenshot and screen-cast software	techsmith.com/jing

Tool	Description	Available from
Lapse It	Time-lapse video maker for iOS and Android	lapseit.com
LEGO Movie Maker	Stop-motion video maker	itunes.apple.com
Make Beliefs Comix	Comic strip generator	makebeliefscomix.com
Mozilla Webmaker	Open-source web building tools	webmaker.org
Open Badge Designer	Open-source tool for creating digital badges	openbadges.me
Scratch	Game design and animation application	scratch.mit.edu
Screencast-o-matic	Screen recording tool	screencast-o-matic.com
Storybird	Visual storytelling tool	storybird.com
Tellagami	Android and iOS app for avatar animation	tellagami.com
ThingLink	Interactive image creator	thinglink.com
Toon Boom	Animation and storyboarding software	toonboom.com
Toondoo	Comic strip and cartoon generator	toondoo.com
Toontastic	Digital storytelling tool	launchpadtoys.com
Twine	Open-source interactive storytelling tool	twinery.org
ZooBurst	Interactive 3-D storytelling tool	zooburst.com
Zunal	WebQuest generator	zunal.com

References

Abrahamson, Craig Eilert. 1998. "Storytelling as a Pedagogical Tool in Higher Education." *Education* 118 (3): 440–451.

Adams, Suellen S. 2009. "The Case for Video Games in Libraries." *Library Review* 58 (3): 196–202. doi:10.1108/00242530910942045.

American Association of School Librarians. 2007. *Standards for the 21st-Century Learner*. Chicago: American Library Association. http://www.ala.org/aasl/standards.

American Library Association. 1989. *Presidential Committee on Information Literacy. Final Report*. Chicago: American Library Association. http://www.ala.org/acrl/publications/whitepapers/presidential.

American Library Association. 2015. "Equity of Access." *American Library Association*. http://www.ala.org/advocacy/access/equityofaccess.

Apperley, Thomas, and Christopher Walsh. 2012. "What Digital Games and Literacy Have in Common: A Heuristic for Understanding Pupils' Gaming Literacy." *Literacy* 46 (3): 115–122. doi:10.1111/j.1741-4369.2012.00668.x.

Baker, Frank W. 2012. "Visual Literacy." In *Media Literacy in the K-12 Classroom*, 41–71. Arlington, VA: International Society for Technology in Education.

Bhabha, Homi K. 1994. *The Location of Culture*. New York: Routledge.

Bourdaa, Melanie. 2014. "This Is Not Marketing. This Is HBO: Branding HBO with Transmedia Storytelling." *Networking Knowledge* 7 (1): 18–25. http://ojs.meccsa.org.uk/index.php/netknow/article/view/328.

Brokaw, Tom. 2013. "Steven Spielberg." *Time*, April 18. http://time100.time.com/2013/04/18/time-100/slide/steven-spielberg/.

Brough, Melissa M., and Sangita Shresthova. 2012. "Fandom Meets Activism: Rethinking Civic and Political Participation." *Transformative Works and Cultures* 10. doi:10.3983/twc.2012.0303.

Cassell, J., and K. Ryokai. 2001. "Making Space for Voice: Technologies to Support Children's Fantasy and Storytelling." *Personal and Ubiquitous Computing* 5 (3): 169–190. doi:10.1007/PL00000018.

The Child Development Institute. 2013. *When a Child Pretends: Understanding Pretend Play*. Bronxville, NY: Sarah Lawrence College. https://www.sarahlawrence.edu/cdi/media/pdf/SLC_WhenAChildPretends_Booklet.pdf.

Coiro, Julie. 2003. "Reading Comprehension in the Internet: Expanding Our Understanding of Reading Comprehension to Encompass New Literacies." *Reading Teacher* 56 (5): 458–464.

Cooper, Patricia. 2005. "Literacy Learning and Pedagogical Purpose in Vivian Paley's 'Storytelling Curriculum.'" *Journal of Early Childhood Literacy* 5 (3): 229–251. doi:10.1177/1468798405058686.

Corporation of Public Broadcasting. 2011. "Findings from Ready To Learn, 2005–2010." The contents of this report were developed under a grant, #PRU 295A050003 and #PRU 295B050003, from the U.S. Department of Education. http://www.cpb.org/rtl/FindingsFromReadyToLearn2005–2010.pdf.

Cropley, Arthur. 2006. "In Praise of Convergent Thinking." *Creativity Research Journal* 18 (3): 391–404. doi:10.1207/s15326934crj1803_13.

Csikszentmihalyi, Mihaly. 1990. *Flow: The Psychology of Optimal Experience*. New York: Harper & Row.

Davis, Charles H. 2013. "Audience Value and Transmedia Products." In *Media Innovations: A Multidisciplinary Study of Change*, edited by Tanja Storsul and Arne H. Krumsvik, 175–190. Goteberg: Nordicom.

Dena, Christy. 2004. "Current State of Cross Media Storytelling: Preliminary Observations for Future Design." Delivered by Monique de Haas at "Crossmedia Communication in the Dynamic Knowledge Society" Networking Session, European Information Systems Technologies Event. The Hague.

Doloughan, Fiona J. 2011. *Contemporary Narrative: Textual Production, Multimodality and Multiliteracies*. New York: Bloomsbury Publishing.

Driscoll, Marcy P. 2005. *Psychology of Learning for Instruction*. 3rd ed. Boston: Pearson Education.

Elmborg, James. 2011. "Libraries as the Spaces Between Us: Recognizing and Valuing the Third Space." *Reference & User Services Quarterly* 50 (4): 338–350.

Entertainment Software Association. 2015. "Essential Facts about the Computer and Video Game Industry." http://www.theesa.com/wp-content/uploads/2015/04/ESA-Essential-Facts-2015.pdf.

Ericsson, K. Anders, and Andreas C. Lehman. 1999. "Expertise." In *Encyclopedia of Creativity*, edited by Mark A. Runco and Steven R. Pritzker, 695–707. San Diego, CA: Academic Press.

Ferreiraa, Soraia, Artur Pimenta Alvesa, and Célia Quicob. 2014. "Location Based Transmedia Storytelling in Social Media–Peter's TravelPlot Porto Case Study." *ENTER 2014 Conference on Information and Communication Technologies in Tourism RESEARCH NOTES*. Dublin.

Fisher, Kenn. 2010. *Technology-Enabled Active Learning Environments: An Appraisal*. CELE Exchange, Centre for Effective Learning Environments, OECD Publishing. doi:10.1787/20727925.

Freire, Paulo. 1985. *The Politics of Education*. Westport, CT: Bergin & Garvey Publishers.

Freire, Paulo. 2000. *Pedagogy of the Oppressed*. Translated by Myra Bergman Ramos. 30th Anniversary ed. New York: Bloomsbury Academic.

The Fullbright Company. 2013. *Gone Home*. Video Game. http://www.gonehomegame.com/.

Gee, James Paul. 2007a. *Social Linguistics and Literacies: Ideology in Discourses*. London: Routledge.

Gee, James Paul. 2007b. *What Video Games Have to Teach Us about Learning and Literacy*. 2nd ed. New York: Palgrave Macmillan Trade.

Gee, James Paul. 2012. "Digital Games and Libraries." *Knowledge Quest* 41 (1): 60–64.

Golick, Jill, and Julie Strassman-Cohn. 2012–2014. *Ruby Skye P. I.* Web Series. Directed by Kelly Harms. Produced by Jill Golick and Kelly Harms. http://rubyskyepi.com/.

Gruenewald, David A. 2003. "The Best of Both Worlds: A Critical Pedagogy of Place." *Educational Researcher* 32 (4): 3–12. doi:10.3102/0013189X032004003.

Gutierrez, Kris, Betsy Rymes, and Joanne Larson. 1995. "Script, Counterscript, and Underlife in the Classroom: James Brown versus Brown vs. Board of Education." *Harvard Educational Review* 65 (3): 445–471.

Harster, Jerome C. 2003. "What Do We Mean by Literacy Now?" *Voices from the Middle* 10 (3): 8–11. http://www.ncte.org/journals/vm.

Herr-Stephenson, Meryl Alper, Erin Reilly, and Henry Jenkins. 2013. *T Is for Transmedia: Learning through Transmedia Play*. Los Angeles and New York:

USC Annenberg Innovation Lab and The Joan Ganz Cooney Center at Sesame Workshop. http://www.annenberglab.com/viewresearch/46.

Hovious, Amanda. 2014. "Inanimate Alice: Born Digital." *Teacher Librarian* 42 (2): 42–46.

Hung, Woei, and Richard Van Eck. 2010. "Aligning Problem Solving and Gameplay: A Model for Future Research and Design." In *Interdisciplinary Models and Tools for Serious Games: Emerging Concepts and Future Directions*, edited by Richard Van Eck, 227–263. Hershey, PA: Information Science Reference.

International Society for Technology in Education. 2007. *ISTE Standards for Students*. Arlington, VA: International Society for Technology in Education. http://www.iste.org/standards/iste-standards/standards-for-students.

Jenkins, Christine A. 2000. "The History of Youth Services Librarianship: A Review of the Research Literature." *Libraries & Culture* 35 (1): 103–140.

Jenkins, Henry. 2003. "Transmedia Storytelling." *Technology Review*, January 15: online. http://www.technologyreview.com/news/401760/transmedia-storytelling/.

Jenkins, Henry. 2004. "Game Design as Narrative Architecture." In *First Person: New Media as Story, Performance, and Game*, edited by Noah Wardrip-Fruin and Pat Harrigan, 118–30. Cambridge, MA: MIT Press.

Jenkins, Henry. 2006. *Convergence Culture: Where Old and New Media Collide*. New York University Press: New York.

Jenkins, Henry. 2007. "Narrative Spaces." In *Space Time Play: Computer Games, Architecture, and Urbanism: The Next Level*, edited by Friedrich von Borries, Steffen P. Walz, Matthias Botger, Drew Davidson, Heather Kelley, and Julian Kuchlich, 56–63. Boston: Springer Science & Business Media.

Jenkins, Henry. 2009a. *Confronting the Challenges of Participatory Culture: Media Education for the 21st Century*. John D. and Catherine T. MacArthur Foundation Reports on Digital Media and Learning, Cambridge, MA: MIT Press. https://mitpress.mit.edu/sites/default/files/titles/free_download/9780262513623_Confronting_the_Challenges.pdf.

Jenkins, Henry. 2009b. "The Revenge of the Origami Unicorn: Seven Principles of Transmedia Storytelling." *Confessions of an Aca-Fan*. December 12. http://henryjenkins.org/2009/12/the_revenge_of_the_origami_uni.html.

Jenkins, Henry. 2012. " 'Cultural Acupuncture': Fan Activism and the Harry Potter Alliance." *Transformative Works and Cultures* 10. doi:10.3983/twc.2012.0305.

Jewitt, Carey. 2006. *Technology, Literacy and Learning: A Multimodal Approach*. New York: Routledge.

Jewitt, Carey. 2008. "Multimodality and Literacy in School Classrooms." *Review of Research in Education* 32 (1): 241–267. doi:10.3102/0091732X07310586.

Jonassen, David H. 2000. "Toward a Design Theory of Problem Solving." *Educational Technology Research and Development* 48 (4): 63–85.

Kalantzis, Mary, and Bill Cope. 2012. "Literacies: Chapter 6: Critical Literacy Pedagogy: Supporting Material." *New Learning: Transformational Designs for Pedagogy and Assessment*. http://newlearningonline.com/literacies/chapter-6.

Kiley, Rachel, Kate Rorick, and Anne Toole. 2012–2014. *The Lizzie Bennet Diaries*. Transmedia Web Series. Directed by Bernie Su. Produced by Bernie Su and Hank Green. Performed by Ashley Clements.

Kress, Gunther. 2010. *Multimodality: A Social Semiotic Approach to Contemporary Communication*. New York: Routledge.

Lankshear, Colin. 1997. *Changing Literacies*. Bristol, PA: Open University Press.

Lankshear, Colin, and Michele Knobel. 2006. *New Literacies*. 2nd ed. Maidenhead, UK: Open University Press.

Lave, Jean, and Etienne Wenger. 2003. *Situated Learning: Legitimate Peripheral Participation*. Cambridge, UK: Cambridge University Press.

Lenhart, Amanda, Joseph Kahne, Ellen Middaugh, Alexandra Rankin Macgill, Chris Evans, and Jessica Vitak. 2008. *Teens, Video Games, and Civics*. Civic Engagement Research Group, Washington, D.C.: Pew Internet & American Life Project. http://www.pewinternet.org/2008/09/16/teens-video-games-and-civics/.

Leu, Donald J. 2002. "The New Literacies: Research on Reading Instruction with the Internet." In *What Research Has to Say about Reading Instruction*, edited by Alan E. Farstrup and S. Jay Samuels, 310–336. Newark: International Reading Association. http://www.sp.uconn.edu/~djleu/newlit.html.

Leu, Donald J., Elena Forzani, Chris Rhoads, Cheryl Maykel, Clint Kennedy, and Nicole Timbrell. 2015. "The New Literacies of Online Research and Comprehension: Rethinking the Reading Achievement Gap." *Reading Research Quarterly* 50 (1): 37–59. doi:10.1002/rrq.85.

Leu, Donald J., Charles K. Kinzer, Julie L. Coiro, Jill Castek, and Laurie A. Henry. 2013. "New Literacies: A Dual-Level Theory of the Changing Nature of Literacy, Instruction and Assessment." In *Theoretical Models and Processes of Reading*, edited by Donna Alverman, Robert B. Ruddell, and Norman Unrau, 1150–1181. Newark: International Reading Association.

Loertscher, David V., and Carol Koechlin. 2014. "Climbing to Excellence—Defining Characteristics of Successful Learning Commons." *Knowledge Quest* 42 (4): E1–E10.

Loertscher, David V., Leslie Preddy, and Bill Derry. 2013. "Makerspaces in the School Library Learning Commons and the uTEC Maker Model." *Teacher Librarian* 41 (2): 48–51.

Loertscher, David V., and Blanche Woolls. 2014. "Transmedia Storytelling as an Education Tool." *IFLA WLIC 2014—Lyon—Libraries, Citizens, Societies: Confluence for Knowledge*. Lyon, France. http://library.ifla.org/881/1/168-loertscher-en.pdf.

Magno, Carlo. 2010. "The Role of Metacognitive Skills in Developing Critical Thinking." *Metacognition and Learning* 5 (2): 137–156.

McGonigal, Jane. 2008. "Why I Love Bees: A Case Study in Collective Intelligence Gaming." In *The Ecology of Games: Connecting Youth, Games, and Learning*, edited by Katie Salen, 199–228. Cambridge, MA: The MIT Press. doi:10.1162/dmal.9780262693646.199.

McLaughlin, Maureen, and Glenn L. DeVoogd. 2004. *Critical Literacy: Enhancing Students' Comprehension of Text*. New York: Scholastic.

Mills, Kathy A. 2011. "Shrek Meets Vygotsky: Rethinking Adolescents' Multimodal Literacy Practices in Schools." *Journal of Adolescent & Adult Literacy* 54 (1): 35–45. doi:10.1598/JAAL.54.1.4.

Moje, Elizabeth Birr, Kathryn McIntosh Ciechanowski, Katherine Kramer, Lindsay Ellis, Rosario Carrillo, and Tehani Collazo. 2004. "Working toward Third Space in Content Area Literacy: An Examination of Everyday Funds of Knowledge and Discourse." *Reading Research Quarterly* 39 (1): 38–70.

Murray, Janet. 2004. "From Game-Story to Cyberdrama." In *First Person: New Media as Story, Performance and Game*, edited by Noah Wardrip-Fruin and Pat Harrigan, 2–11. Cambridge, MA: MIT Press.

NAMLE. 2015. "Media Literacy Defined." *National Association of Media Literacy Education*. http://namle.net/publications/media-literacy-definitions/.

National Governors Association Center for Best Practices, and Council of Chief State School Officers. 2010. *Common Core State Standards*. Washington, DC: Authors. http://www.corestandards.org/.

NCTE. 2008. "NCTE Position Statement on Multimodal Literacies." National Council of Teachers of English. August 18. http://www.ncte.org/positions/statements/multimodalliteracies.

New London Group. 1996. "A Pedagogy of Multiliteracies: Designing Social Futures." *Harvard Educational Review* 66 (1): 60–92.

O'Brien, David, and Cassandra Scharber. 2008. "Digital Literacies Go to School: Potholes and Possibilities." *Journal of Adolescent & Adult Literacy* 52 (1): 66–68. doi:10.1598/JAAL.52.1.7.

Oldenburg, Ray. 1999. *The Great Good Place*. New York: Marlowe & Company.

Oldenburg, Ray. 2001. *Celebrating the Third Place: Inspiring Stories about the "Great Good Places" at the Heart of Our Communities*. New York: Marlowe & Company.

Ormrod, Jeanne Ellis. 2012. *Human Learning*. 6th ed. Boston: Pearson Education, Inc.

Paley, Vivian Gussin. 1990. *The Boy Who Would Be a Helicopter*. Cambridge, MA: Harvard University Press.

Pallotta, Tommy. 2010. *Collapsus: Energy Risk Conspiracy*. Directed by Tommy Pallotta. Produced by Bruno Felix and Femke Wolting. http://www.collapsus.com/.

Parr, Michaelann, and Terry Campbell. 2012. *Balanced Literacy Essentials: Weaving Theory into Practice for Successful Instruction in Reading, Writing, and Talk*. Markham, Ontario, Canada: Pembroke Publishers.

Pool, Carol R. 1997. "A New Digital Literacy: A Conversation with Paul Gilster." *Educational Leadership* 55 (3): 6–11.

Pratten, Robert. 2011. "Getting Started in Transmedia Storytelling." *Transmedia Storyteller*. January 25. http://www.tstoryteller.com/getting-started-in-transmedia-storytelling.

Prensky, Marc. 2006. *Don't Bother Me, Mom, I'm Learning: How Computer and Video Games Are Preparing Your Kids for 21st Century Success and How You Can Help*. New York: Paragon House.

Pullinger, Kate, and Chris Joseph. 2005–. *Inanimate Alice*. Interactive Fiction. Produced by Ian Harper. http://inanimatealice.com.

Raybourn, Elaine M. "A New Paradigm for Serious Games: Transmedia Learning for More Effective Training and Education." *Journal of Computational Science* 5 (3): 471–481.

Rieber, Lloyd P. 1996. "Seriously Considering Play: Designing Interactive Learning Environments Based on the Blending of Microworlds, Simulations, and Games." *Educational Technology Research and Development* 44 (2): 43–58.

Rose, Frank. 2015. "How to Harness the Power of Immersive Media." February 9. Accessed March 6, 2015. http://www.deepmediaonline.com/deepmedia/2015/02/strategy-business-how-to-harness-the-power-of-immersive-media.html.

Roskos, Kathleen, and James Christie. 2001. "Examining the Play-Literacy Interface: A Critical Review and Future Directions." *Journal of Early Childhood Literacy* 1 (1): 59–89.

Roth, Christian, Peter Vorderer, and Christoph Klimmt. 2009. "The Motivational Appeal of Interactive Storytelling: Towards a Dimensional Model of the User Experience." In *Second Joint International Conference on Interactive Digital Storytelling: Proceedings*, edited by Ido A. Iurgel, Nelson Zagalo, and Petta Paolo, 38–43. Guimarães, Portugal: Springer Berlin Heidelberg.

Saldre, Maarja, and Peeter Torop. 2012. "Transmedia Space." In *Crossmedia Innovations: Texts, Markets, Institutions*, edited by Indrek Ibrus and Carlos A. Scolari, 25–44. New York: Peter Lang.

Sanders, Jennifer, and Peggy Albers. 2010. "Multimodal Literacies: An Introduction." In *Literacies, the Arts and Multimodalities*, edited by Jennifer Sanders and Peggy Albers, 1–25. Urbana: National Council of Teachers of English.

Shute, Valerie J., Llloyd Rieber, and Richard Van Eck. 2012. "Games . . . and . . . Learning." In *Trends and Issues in Instructional Design and Technology*, edited by Robert Reiser and John Dempsey, 321–332. Upper Saddle River, NJ: Pearson Education.

Solorzano, Daniel G., and Tara J. Yasso. 2002. "Critical Race Methodology: Counter-Storytelling as an Analytical Framework for Education Research." *Qualitative Inquiry* 8 (1): 23–44. doi: 10.1177/107780040200800103.

Spielberg, Steven. 2012. *Steven Spielberg on How Lawrence of Arabia Inspired Him to Make Movies*. Interview by American Film Institute (December 27). https://youtu.be/ayJLeVDOCZ0.

Squire, Kurt D. 2008. "Video-Game Literacy: A Literacy of Expertise." In *Handbook of Research on New Literacies*, edited by Julie Coiro, Michele Knobel, Colin Lankshear, and Donald J. Leu, 635–670. New York: Routledge.

Starko, Alan. 2013. "Creativity on the Brink?" *Creativity Now* 70 (5): 54–56.

Steinkuehler, Connie. 2010. "Video Games and Digital Literacies." *Journal of Adolescent & Adult Literacy* 54 (1): 61–63.

Street, Brian V. 1995. *Social Literacies*. London: Longman.

Su, Bernie, and Kate Rorick. 2014. *The Secret Diary of Lizzie Bennet*. New York: Touchstone.

Sung, Ki. 2015. "Gone Home: A Video Game as a Tool for Teaching Critical Thinking Skills." *Mind/Shift*. January 16. http://blogs.kqed.org/mindshift/2015/01/gone-home-a-video-game-as-a-tool-for-teaching-critical-thinking/.

Sweetapple, Matthew, and Elaine Sweetapple. 2010. *Rockford's Rock Opera*. Interactive Fiction. http://www.rockfordsrockopera.com.

Tillett, Barbara. 2004. *What Is FRBR? A Conceptual Model for the Bibliographic Universe*. Washington, D.C.: Library of Congress Cataloging Distribution Service. http://www.loc.gov/cds/downloads/FRBR.PDF.

Vukadin, Ana. 2014. "Bits and Pieces of Information: Bibliographic Modeling of Transmedia." *Cataloging & Classification Quarterly* 52 (3): 285–302. doi: 10.1080/01639374.2013.879976.

Walker, Jill. 2004. "Distributed Narrative: Telling Stories Across Networks." Paper presented at *Association of Internet Researchers 5th Annual Conference: Ubiquity*.

Wallas, Graham. 1926. *The Art of Thought*. Reprint, Kent, England: Solis Press, 2014.

Walt Disney World. n.d. *Disney's Hollywood Studios Attractions*. https://disneyworld.disney.go.com/attractions/hollywood-studios/star-tours/.

Weiler, Lance. 2011. *Robot Heart Stories*. Transmedia Storytelling Project. Produced by Janine Saunders. http://robotsjourney.tumblr.com/ /.

Wohlwend, Karen. 2008. "Play as a Literacy of Possibilities: Expanding Meanings in Practices, Materials, and Spaces." *Language Arts* 86 (2): 127–136.

Wolf, Werner. 2006. "Introduction: Frames, Framings, and Framing Borders in Literature and Other Media." In *Framing Borders in Literature and Other Media*, edited by Werner Wolf and Walter Bernhart, 1–42. Amsterdam: Rodopi.

Wookieepedia: The Star Wars Wiki. 2015. http://starwars.wikia.com.

Zimmerman, Barry J. 2002. "Becoming a Self-Regulated Learner: An Overview." *Theory into Practice* 41 (2): 64–70.

Index